SPIRALIZER 1
Jennifer Wittman

Healthy, Delicious and Creativity Meals through Your Spiralizer, Easy Rapid Weight Loss, Regain Your Optimal Health With The Top Best 200 Spiralizer Recipes

Creative Healthy Meals For Rapid Weight Loss

Copyright 2017 by Jennifer Wittman All rights reserved.

In no way is it legal to reproduce, duplicate, or transmit any part of this document in either electronic means or in printed format. Recording of this publication is strictly prohibited and any storage of this document is not allowed unless with written permission from the publisher. All rights reserved.

The information provided herein is stated to be truthful and consistent, in that any liability, in terms of inattention or otherwise, by any usage or abuse of any policies, processes, or directions contained within is the solitary and utter responsibility of the recipient reader. Under no circumstances will any legal responsibility or blame be held against the publisher for any reparation, damages, or monetary loss due to the information herein, either directly or indirectly.

Respective authors own all copyrights not held by the publisher.

The information herein is offered for informational purposes solely, and is universal as so. The presentation of the information is without contract or any type of guarantee assurance.

The trademarks that are used are without any consent, and the publication of the trademark is without permission or backing by the trademark owner. All trademarks and brands within this book are for clarifying purposes only and are the owned by the owners themselves, not affiliated with this document.

Table of Contents

SPIRALIZER RECIPES 1

Copyright 2017 by Jennifer Wittman All rights reserved. 3

Introduction 12

CHAPTER 1 BENEFITS OF A SPIRALIZER 14

HOW TO ASSAMBLE THE SPIRALIZER 15

Chapter 2 POULTRY SPIRALIZER RECIPES 16

- Delicious Zucchini with Scrambled Eggs 16
- Cheesy Scrambled Avocado Eggs 17
- Scallion Avocado Beet Omelet 18
- Garlic Zucchini & Kale Frittata 19
- Cheesy Zucchini & Spinach Frittata 20
- Tomato Sweet Potato with Eggs 21
- Cheesy Onion Sweet Potato & Eggs 22
- Garlic Spinach & Chicken with Eggs 23
- Delicious Potato with Eggs 24
- Sweet Potato & Zucchini with Eggs 25
- Cilantro Chicken Zucchini with Eggs 26
- Yummy Fried Eggs Sweet Potato & Chicken 27
- Black Peppers Fried Eggs Jicama 29
- Soy Sauce Zucchini Fried Eggs 30
- Mozzarella Zucchini with Fried Eggs 31
- Fruity Sweet Potato Buns 32
- Butter Sweet Potato Buns Sandwich 33
- Chicken Zucchini Buns Sandwich 35
- Yummy Zucchini Patties & Sweet Potato 37
- Almond Cumin Carrot & Zucchini Patties 39

Delight Spinach Sweet Potato Muffins 40

Cilantro Carrot & Zucchini Loaf 41

Pumpkin Spice Sweet Potato Waffles 42

Garlic Egg Parsnip Waffles 43

Cheddar Potato Pancakes 44

Honey Zucchini Pancakes 46

Avocado Sweet Potato & Chicken Rolls 47

Tapioca Zucchini & Chicken Pizza 48

Scallion Zucchini & Egg Bake.. 50

Garlic Spicy Zucchini Chicken 51

Tamari Zucchini with Chicken... 52

Eggplant Zucchini & Chicken... 53

Chili Chicken With Broccoli & Zucchini.. 54

Garlic Chicken Zucchini & Kale 55

Tomatoes Zucchini & Chicken... 56

Chicken Zucchini & Radish 58

Zucchini with Spinach & Chicken 59

Black Pepper Zucchini with Spinach & Chicken 60

Chicken Bake With Zucchini, Mushrooms 61

Chicken With Kale &Yellow Squash 63

Chicken With Yellow Squash &Tomatoes 64

Pumpkin Puree Chicken With Yellow Squash 65

Tasty Sweet Potato with Asparagus & Chicken.. 66

Scallion Chicken Sweet Potato.. 67

Ginger Chicken With Veggies& Sweet Potato 69

Rosemary Artichokes & Chicken With Sweet Potato 70

Brussels Sprout Chicken & Sweet Potato 72

Chicken Curry & Sweet Potato 74

Chicken Casserole Black Beans & Sweet Potato 76

Parsnip & Sweet Potato Chicken Casserole 78

Rosemary Parsnip & Carrot with Chicken 79

Garlic Parsnip with Capers & Chicken 80

Cheddar Thyme Broccoli with Chicken 82

Delicious Chicken Mixed Veggies 83

Garlic Turkey Sweet Potato with Spinach 84

Bell Pepper Zucchini Turkey 86

Arugula Turkey & Sweet Potato with 87

Mushroom Zucchini Turkey 88

Turkey Meatballs With Zucchini Spinach 90

Tomatoes Duck Zucchini 91

Chapter 3 SPIRALIZER SALAD RECIPES 93

Pecan Apple & Carrot Salad 93

Parmesan Apple & Scallion Salad 94

Walnut Apple & Basil Salad 95

Spinach Apple & Greens Salad 96

Yummy Pear & Brussels Sprout Salad 97

Yogurt Dill Cucumber Salad 98

Cucumber & Melon Salad 99

Dijon Mustard Cucumber & Egg Salad 100

Walnut Cucumber & Tomato Salad 101

Spinach Cucumber & Asparagus Salad 102

Peanut Butter Cucumber & Carrot Salad 103

Cucumber, Onion & Pimentos Salad 104

Honey Cucumber & Onion Salad 105

Cucumber & Avocado Beet Salad ... 106

Ginger Carrot Salad in Basil Sauce ... 107

Chickpeas Zucchini & Carrot Salad ... 108

Raisins Zucchini & Berries Salad ... 109

Pomegranate Zucchini Pear Salad ... 110

Honey Zucchini & Cranberry Salad ... 111

Almond Zucchini Salad in Mango Sauce ... 112

Spicy Almond Butter Sauce Zucchini Salad ... 113

Kale Broccoli Zucchini Salad ... 114

Delicious Zucchini & Cucumber Salad in Sweet & Spicy Sauce ... 115

Parsley Cabbage Salad ... 116

Kale Cabbage & Carrot Salad ... 117

Crumbled Fetta Cheese Honey Beet Salad ... 118

Sesame Beet & Avocado Salad ... 119

Fresh Mint Beet & Cashew Salad ... 120

Pecans Beet & Cherry Salad ... 121

Yummy Beet & Orange Salad ... 122

Chili Zucchini & Corn Salad ... 123

Kidney Beans Zucchini Salad ... 124

Cumin Carrot, Zucchini & Chickpeas Salad ... 125

Pine Nuts Zucchini & Quinoa Salad ... 126

Delicious Zucchini & Chicken Salad ... 127

Cashews Zucchini, Carrot & Chicken Salad ... 129

Garlic Zucchini, Cucumber & Chicken Salad ... 130

Zucchini & Turkey Salad ... 132

Soy Sauce Steak Salad With Carrot, Cucumber ... 133

Radishes Zucchini & Steak Salad ... 135

Walnut Zucchini & Salmon Salad ... 136

Zucchini, Cucumber & Salmon Salad ... 138

Yummy Cod Salad ... 139

Zucchini & Sardine Salad ... 140

Ginger Zucchini & Shrimp Salad ... 142

CHAPTER 4 STEW & SOUP SPIRALIZER RECIPES ... 144

Yummy Zucchini & Roasted Tomato Soup ... 144

Onion Zucchini & Bok Choy Soup ... 145

Scallion Zucchini & Asparagus Soup ... 147

Healthy Radish & Mushroom Soup ... 148

Soy Sauce Zucchini & Tofu Soup ... 149

Thyme Turnip & Lentil Soup ... 150

Chili Butternut Squash & Cannelini Beans Soup ... 152

Carrot & Cannellini Beans Soup ... 153

Ginger Sweet Potato & Chickpeas Soup ... 155

Carrots Zucchini & Bacon Soup ... 156

Garlic Mixed Veggies & Bacon Soup ... 158

Coconut Curried Zucchini Chicken Soup ... 159

Jalapeno Zucchini, Salsa & Chicken Soup ... 161

Mushroom Zucchini, Yellow Squash & Chicken Soup ... 162

Carrots Yellow Squash & Chicken Soup ... 163

Basil Carrot & Chicken Soup ... 164

Celery Carrot & Chicken Soup ... 165

Cilantro Curried Turnip & Chicken Soup ... 167

Rosemary Rutabaga & Turkey Soup ... 168

Delicious Zucchini & Turkey Soup ... 169

Sesame Oil Zucchini, Seaweed & Turkey Soup ... 170

Cumin Yellow Squash & Turkey Meatballs Soup 171

Mushroom Yellow Squash & Beef Soup 173

Ground Beef Soup & Zucchini 174

Black Olive Zucchini & Meatballs Soup 176

Ginger Zucchini & Lamb Soup 178

Garlic Sweet Potato & Ground Pork Soup 180

Cilantro Ginger Radish & Pork Meatballs Soup 181

Onion Carrot & Sausage Soup 183

Pesto Zucchini & Sausage Soup 184

Tasty Salmon Fillets Soup & Zucchini 186

Jalapeno Zucchini & Herring Soup 187

Ginger Zucchini & Shrimp Soup 188

Nutritious Mixed Veggie Stew 189

Garlic Onion Rutabaga & Beans Stew 190

Cumin Thyme Butternut Squash & Beans Stew 192

Yummy Zucchini & Chicken Stew 193

Celery Rutabaga & Beef Stew 195

Garlic Tamari Zucchini, Squash & Beef Stew 196

Parsley Zucchini & Lamb Stew 198

Garlic Rosemary Potato & Cod Stew 200

Kernels Zucchini & Shrimp Stew 201

CHAPTER 6 SPIRALIZER MEAT & SEAFOOD RECIPES 202

Zucchini with Spinach & Steak 202

Coconut Zucchini Steak 204

Ginger Carrot with Grouper Fillets 205

Cod Fillets Spinach Zucchini 206

Delicious Zucchini, Chard & Cod Parcel 208

Garlic Ground Beef & Zucchini	209
Avocado Zucchini Ground Beef	210
Ground Beef Mushrooms Basil & Zucchini	211
Rosemary Ground Beef Zucchini	212
Mushrooms Onion Haddock Fillets Zucchini	214
Butternut Squash with Broccoli & Herring	215
Lemon Garlic Zucchini with Salmon	217
Yummy Yellow Squash Curry with Beef & Zucchini	218
Curry Kale Steak & Yellow Squash	220
Salmon Zucchini with Spinach	221
Soy Sauce Zucchini with Mushrooms & Salmon	223
Delicious Salmon Casserole & Zucchini	224
Yellow Squash with Beef Meatballs	225
Asparagus Sirloin Steak & Sweet Potato	227
Veggies Mixed Beef & Sweet Potato	229
Coconut Turnip & Salmon Curry	230
Sardines Zucchini	231
Rosemary Tuna Asparagus Zucchini	233
Sweet Potato with Ground Beef	235
Ginger Sweet Potato with Beef Meatballs	236
Chili Zucchini with Tomatoes & Shrimp	238
Honey Broccoli Zucchini Shrimp	239
Parsley Zucchini with Asparagus & Shrimp	240
Delicious Sweet Potato & Beef Meatballs Curry	241
Thyme Cabbage with Ground Beef	243
Sweet & Sour Balsamic Cabbage Ground Beef	244
Garlic Carrot with Steak	245

Soy Sauce Zucchini Prawns 246

Chili Sweet Potato with Calms 247

Hoisin Sauce Broccoli Steak 248

Cumin Celeriac with Ground Lamb 250

Garlic Lamb Cutlets Sweet Potato 252

Yummy Zucchini with Lamb Cutlets 253

Garlic Scallops Zucchini 254

Scallops Zucchini with Spinach 255

Delight Apple with Spinach & Scallops 257

Chili Zucchini Lobster 258

Lamb Meatballs With Zucchini 259

Garlic Lamb Muffins With Zucchini 261

Ginger Honey Turnip Tenderloin Pork 263

Butter Lobster With Sweet Potato 265

Zucchini Onion Mussels 267

Garlic Crab With Butternut Squash 268

Tamari Ginger Cabbage with Ground Pork 269

Conclusion 271

Introduction

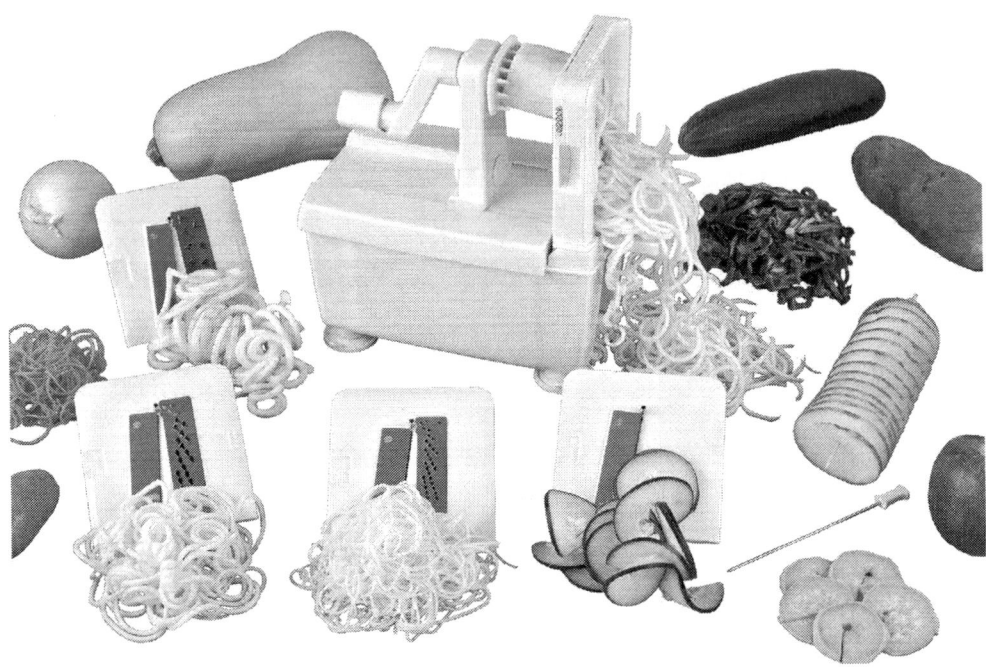

I want to thank you and congratulate you for downloading the book, "SPIRALIZER RECIPES: Healthy, Delicious and Creativity Meals through Your Spiralizer, Easy Rapid Weight Loss, Regain Your Optimal Health With the Top Best 200 Spiralizer Recipes"

The spiralizer is a very useful tool used to slice and cut veggies quickly and easily. Turning this kitchen chore into a task that's done in the blink of an eye!

As with the advent of newer kitchen technologies and appliances, cooking has never been easier. The preparation time required to make and create food, especially healthy options is now cut down.

Vegetables are an integral part of healthy diets. However, it's not as appealing to all members of the family – looking at the kids in particular!

This means that people are less motivated to make healthy foods if everyone isn't excited about it.

The spiralizer is a simple tool for prepping vegetables, also known as the vegetable-noodle maker or the spiral vegetable slicer. Spiralizers can create strings from tough vegetables such as carrots, zucchinis, potatoes and much more. In fact, these noodle-like strings can be used as a cooking alternative to regular noodles and spaghetti.

Cutting back on carbs and filling your diet with veggies and fruits is easy with a spiralizer!

Put a personal twist into your recipes by using spiralized veggies and fruit. It's also a great way to make recipes healthier and filled with more nutrients.
Once you've gone through this book, you'll have tons of ideas on how to use the spiralizer in creating healthy meals that may as well become your new favorite dishes.

Learn more about how the spiralizer can make your kitchen time easier and save you a ton of time in food preparation!

Thanks again for purchasing this book. I hope you enjoy it!

CHAPTER 1 BENEFITS OF A SPIRALIZER

Saves Time

No need to spend an inordinate amount of time slaving away, cutting up vegetables. You can just let the spiralizer do all the heavy lifting for you. Simply spiralize and add the resultant strings to whatever you're cooking with, and you're set!

A Variety of Blades for Varying Shapes

You can customize the size and shape of your noodle-like strings, thin or thick; noodles or wedged; diced or grated; and more! You'll be stunned at the variety of options available for you to use!

Say 'Bye!' to Knives

If your hand eye coordination is so bad that your knife may as well be as useful as a spoon, say no more. No need to worry about the cutting work if you have a spiralizer!

Uniformness

By using an appliance like the spiralizer, you can get nice and even cuts that you'd never get even from professional cooks. If you're also aiming for the aesthetic appeal, then having sliced products of the same size also helps with food presentation.

Easy Maintenance

The blades used in the spiralizer can be removed and therefore washed after each use. Using a damp cloth for cleaning minor stains also saves you time on washing the blades. Since the appliance does not run on any electricity or batteries, there is no need for it to be serviced.

Of course, that's not all! You'll find out more about the spiralizer once you've gone through this book!

HOW TO ASSAMBLE THE SPIRALIZER

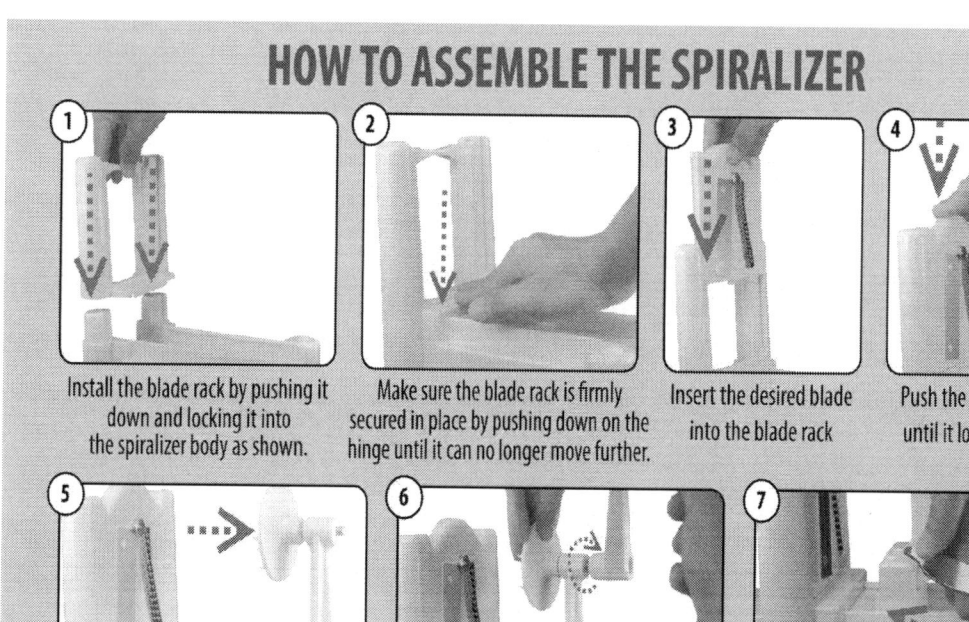

Chapter 2 POULTRY SPIRALIZER RECIPES

Delicious Zucchini with Scrambled Eggs

Time: 25 minutes

Servings: 2

Ingredients:

2 medium zucchinis, spiralized with Blade C

Salt, to taste

1 tablespoon plus ½ teaspoon olive oil, divided

1 tablespoon almond flour

1 garlic clove, minced

3 eggs

Freshly ground black pepper, to taste

¼ cup fresh cilantro leaves, chopped

Directions:

1. In a colander place zucchini noodles and sprinkle with salt.

2. Keep aside for at least 20 minutes.

3. Drain well and pat dry with a paper towel.

4. Meanwhile in a non-stick skillet, mix ½ teaspoon of oil, almond flour and a pinch of salt on medium heat.

5. Cook for about 1 minute, stirring continuously.

6. Remove from heat and keep aside.

7. In another skillet, heat remaining oil on medium heat.

8. Add zucchini noodles and cook for about 1-2 minutes.

9. Transfer the zucchini noodles into a bowl.

10. In the same skillet, add garlic and sauté for about 1 minute.

11. Add eggs and cook, stirring for about 2-3 minutes.

12. Stir in zucchini noodles and cilantro and cook for to about 2 minutes.

13. Top with toasted almond flour and serve.

Cheesy Scrambled Avocado Eggs

Time: 25 minutes

Servings: 2

Ingredients:

1 tablespoon olive oil

2 small potatoes, peeled and spiralized with Blade C

5 eggs

½ cup avocado, peeled, pitted and cubed

½ cup feta cheese, crumbled

2 tablespoons fresh cilantro leaves, chopped

Directions:

1. In a large skillet, heat oil on medium heat.

2. Add potatoes and cook, tossing occasionally for about 8-10 minutes.

3. Add eggs and cubed avocado and cook for about 1-2 minutes, stirring continuously.

4. Add feta and cook stirring for about 1-2 minutes.

5. Garnish with cilantro and serve.

Scallion Avocado Beet Omelet

Time: 30 minutes

Servings: 2

Ingredients:

2 tablespoons olive oil, divided

2 small beets, peeled and spiralized with Blade C

4 large eggs

Salt and freshly ground black pepper, to taste

1 small avocado, peeled, pitted and cubed

1 scallion, chopped

Directions:

1. In a large skillet, heat 1 tablespoon of oil on medium heat.
2. Add beet noodles and cook for about 6-7 minutes.
3. Remove from heat and keep aside.
4. Meanwhile in a bowl, add eggs and seasoning and beat well.
5. In a large frying pan, heat remaining oil on medium heat.
6. Add beaten eggs and with a wooden spoon, spread the eggs towards the edges of pan.
7. Cook for about 1-2 minutes.
8. Place bees and avocado over eggs.
9. Carefully, fold the omelet over the beet noodles and avocado and cook for about 2 minutes.
10. Top with scallions and serve.

Garlic Zucchini & Kale Frittata

Time: 40 minutes

Servings: 4

Ingredients:

1 tablespoon olive oil

1 garlic clove, minced

3 cups fresh kale, trimmed and chopped

1 large zucchini, spiralized with Blade C

Salt and freshly ground black pepper, to taste

12 egg whites, beaten

Directions:

1. Preheat the oven to 375 degrees F.
2. In an oven proof skillet, heat oil on medium heat.
3. Add garlic and sauté for about 1 minute.
4. Add kale and cook for 3-4 minutes or till just wilted.
5. Transfer half of kale into a plate.
6. Place the zucchini noodles over kale evenly and top with remaining kale.
7. Sprinkle with salt and black pepper and spread beaten egg whites over kale evenly.
8. Cook for about 2 minutes.
9. Transfer the skillet into oven and bake for about 15-18 minutes.

Cheesy Zucchini & Spinach Frittata

Time: 40 minutes

Servings: 4

Ingredients:

12 egg whites

Salt and freshly ground black pepper, to taste

2 teaspoons olive oil

1 garlic clove, minced

3 cups fresh baby spinach, chopped

1 large zucchini, spiralized with Blade C

2-ounce feta cheese, crumbled

Directions:

1. Preheat the oven to 375 degrees F.

2. In a large bowl, add egg whites, salt and pepper and beat.

3. In an oven proof skillet, heat oil on medium heat.

4. Add garlic and sauté for about 1 minute.

5. Add spinach and cook for about 2-3 minutes.

6. Transfer half of spinach into a bowl.

7. Place zucchini over spinach evenly.

8. Spread remaining spinach over zucchini and top with egg white mixture evenly.

9. Sprinkle with cheese evenly and slightly push into egg whites.

10. Bake for about 15-20 minutes or till top becomes golden brown.

Tomato Sweet Potato with Eggs

Time: 45 minutes

Servings: 4

Ingredients:

1 tablespoon canola oil

¼ cup white onion, chopped

2 garlic cloves, minced

1 Serrano pepper, seeded and chopped

¼ teaspoon ground cumin

¼ teaspoon red pepper flakes, crushed

2 cups fresh tomatoes, chopped finely

1 large sweet potato, peeled and spiralized with Blade C

Salt and freshly ground Black Pepper, to taste

4 eggs

2 tablespoons fresh basil leaves, chopped

Directions:

1. Preheat the oven to 375 degrees F.

2. In a large skillet, heat oil on medium heat.

3. Add onion and sauté for about 3-4 minutes.

4. Add garlic, Serrano pepper, cumin and red pepper flakes and sauté for about 1 minute.

5. Add tomatoes and cook for about 2-3 minutes.

6. Add sweet potato noodles, salt and black pepper and cook for about 6-7 minutes.

7. Transfer the sweet potato mixture into 4 large ramekins evenly.

8. Crack 1 egg in each ramekin over sweet potato mixture and sprinkle with salt and black pepper.

9. Bake for about 10-15 minutes or till desired doneness.

10. Garnish with basil and serve.

Cheesy Onion Sweet Potato & Eggs

Time: 55 minutes

Servings: 4

Ingredients:

2 tablespoons olive oil

1 onion, sliced

2 garlic cloves, minced

1 large sweet potato, peeled and spiralized with Blade C

8 eggs

Salt and freshly ground black pepper, to taste

2-ounce feta cheese, crumbled

Directions:

1. Preheat the oven to 350 degrees F.

2. In an oven proof skillet, heat oil on medium heat.

3. Add onion and sauté for about 4 minutes.

4. Add garlic and sauté for about 1 minute.

5. Add sweet potato noodles and cook for about 8-10 minutes.

6. Carefully, crack the eggs over sweet potato noodles evenly and sprinkle with salt and black pepper.

7. Bake for about 20 minutes.

8. Remove from oven and sprinkle with cheese evenly.

9. Bake for about 5 minutes more.

Garlic Spinach & Chicken with Eggs

Time: 25 minutes

Servings: 2

Ingredients:

1 tablespoon sunflower oil

½ small white onion, chopped

1 garlic clove, minced

2 medium sweet potatoes, peeled and spiralized with Blade C

¼ teaspoon cayenne pepper

Salt and freshly ground black pepper, to taste

1 cup cooked chicken, chopped finely

2 cups fresh spinach, chopped

2 eggs

Directions:

1. In a large skillet, heat oil on medium heat.
2. Add onion and sauté for about 3-4 minutes.
3. Add garlic and sauté for about 1 minute.
4. Add sweet potato and seasoning and cook for about 4-5 minutes.
5. Add chicken and spinach and cook for about 3-4 minutes.
6. Carefully, crack the eggs over sweet potato mixture.
7. Sprinkle each egg with salt and black pepper.
8. Cover the skillet and cook for about 2-3 minutes or till desired doneness.

Delicious Potato with Eggs

Time: 45 minutes

Servings: 4

Ingredients:

2 tablespoons olive oil

2 large potatoes, peeled and spiralized with Blade C

1 white onion, chopped

2 garlic cloves, minced

Salt and freshly ground black pepper, to taste

8 eggs

Directions:

1. Preheat the oven to 350 degrees F.
2. In a large oven proof skillet, heat oil on medium heat.
3. Add potato noodles and onion and cook for about 8-9 minutes.
4. Add garlic and cook for 1 minute.
5. Carefully, crack the eggs over sweet potato mixture evenly.
6. Transfer the skillet into oven.
7. Bake for about 20-25 minutes.

Sweet Potato & Zucchini with Eggs

Time: 35 minutes

Servings: 2

Ingredients:

2 tablespoons olive oil, divided

1 medium sweet potato, peeled and spiralized with Blade C

1 medium zucchini, spiralized with Blade C

4 eggs

Salt and freshly ground black pepper, to taste

Directions:

1. In a large skillet, heat 1½ tablespoons of oil on medium heat.

2. Add sweet potato noodles and cook for about 3-4 minutes.

3. Add zucchini noodles and cook for about 2-3 minutes.

4. Carefully, make a well in the center of vegetables.

5. Pour remaining oil in the well.

6. Carefully, crack the eggs in the well.

7. Cover the skillet and cook for about 2-3 minutes or till desired doneness.

8. Sprinkle with salt and black pepper and serve.

Cilantro Chicken Zucchini with Eggs

Time: 25 minutes

Servings: 2

Ingredients:

2 tablespoon olive oil, divided

4 small zucchinis, spiralized with Blade C

1 cup cooked chicken breast, cut into bite size pieces

Salt and freshly ground black pepper, to taste

4 eggs

2 tablespoons fresh cilantro leaves, chopped

Directions:

1. In a large skillet, heat 1 tablespoon of oil on medium-high heat.

2. Add zucchini and cook for about 3-4 minutes.

3. Add chicken, salt and black pepper and cook for about 1 minute.

4. Carefully, make 2 wells in the middle of zucchini mixture.

5. Pour remaining oil in the wells.

6. Carefully, crack 2 eggs in each well and sprinkle with salt and black pepper.

7. Cover the skillet and cook for about 2-3 minutes or till desired doneness.

8. Garnish with cilantro and serve.

Yummy Fried Eggs Sweet Potato & Chicken

Time: 40 minutes

Servings: 4

Ingredients:

3 tablespoons olive oil, divided

2 garlic cloves, minced and divided

1 large sweet potato, peeled and spiralized with Blade C

1 small white onion, chopped

1 red bell pepper, seeded and chopped

1 green bell pepper, seeded and chopped

½ teaspoon dried thyme, crushed

¼ teaspoon cayenne pepper

Salt and freshly ground black pepper, to taste

½ cup cooked chicken, shredded

4 eggs

1 tablespoon fresh cilantro, chopped

Directions:

1. In a large skillet, heat 1 tablespoon of oil on medium heat.
2. Add 1 garlic clove and sauté for about 1 minute.
3. Add sweet potato noodles and cook for about 6-8 minutes.
4. Transfer sweet potato noodles into a plate.
5. Meanwhile in another skillet, heat 1 tablespoon of oil on medium heat.
6. Add onion, bell peppers, thyme, remaining garlic and seasoning and cook for about 4-5 minutes.
7. Stir in chicken and transfer the chicken mixture over sweet potato noodles.
8. In a frying pan, heat remaining oil on low heat.
9. Carefully, crack the eggs and cook for about 3-4 minutes.
10. Spoon the hot oil over whites till set, but spoon the oil over yolks only a couple of time.
11. Top the chicken and sweet potato with fried eggs.
12. Garnish with fresh cilantro and serve.

Black Peppers Fried Eggs Jicama

Time: 45 minutes

Servings: 4

Ingredients:

1 large jicama, peeled and spiralized with Blade C

5 tablespoons olive oil, divided

1 teaspoon cayenne pepper

Salt and freshly ground black pepper, to taste

4 large eggs

Directions:

1. Preheat the oven to 400 degrees F.
2. Lightly grease 2 baking sheets.
3. Arrange jicama noodles in prepared baking sheets.
4. Drizzle with 2 tablespoons of oil and sprinkle with spices.
5. Bake for about 30 minutes, flipping once after 15 minutes.
6. Meanwhile in a large frying pan, heat remaining oil on low heat.
7. Carefully, crack the eggs and cook for about 3-4 minutes.
8. Spoon the hot oil over whites till set, but spoon the oil over yolks only a couple of time.
9. Top the jicama with fried eggs and serve immediately.

Soy Sauce Zucchini Fried Eggs

Time: 20 minutes

Servings: 2

Ingredients:

2½ tablespoons extra virgin olive oil, divided

4 eggs

1 large zucchini, spiralized with Blade C

Salt and freshly ground black pepper, to taste

1 tablespoon soy sauce

1 tablespoon fresh parsley, chopped

Directions:

1. In a large frying pan, heat 2 tablespoons of oil on low heat.
2. Carefully, crack the eggs and cook for about 3-4 minutes.
3. Spoon the hot oil over whites till set, but spoon the oil over yolks only a couple of time.
4. Meanwhile place zucchini noodles in a micro wave safe bowl.
5. Sprinkle with salt and black pepper and microwave on High for about 1 minute.
6. Drizzle with ½ tablespoon of oil and soy sauce and microwave for about 1 minute more.
7. Transfer zucchini in a large serving plate and top with fried eggs.

8. Garnish with parsley and serve.

Mozzarella Zucchini with Fried Eggs

Time: 20 minutes
Servings: 2

Ingredients:

2 tablespoons olive oil, divided

1 garlic clove, minced

2 large zucchinis, spiralized with Blade C

¼ teaspoon red pepper flakes, crushed

Salt and freshly ground black pepper, to taste

2 tablespoons mozzarella cheese, grated

4 eggs

Directions:

1. In a large skillet, heat 1 tablespoon of oil on medium heat.
2. Add garlic and sauté for about 1 minute.
3. Add zucchini, red pepper flakes, salt and black pepper and cook for about 3-4 minutes.
4. Transfer the zucchini mixture into 2 large serving plates.
5. Immediately, sprinkle with cheese evenly.
6. Meanwhile in a large frying pan, heat remaining oil on medium heat.
7. Crack the eggs in skillet one by one.
8. Cook for about 2-3 minutes or till desired doneness.

9. Place the eggs over zucchini.
10. Sprinkle each egg with salt and black pepper and serve.

Fruity Sweet Potato Buns

Time: 25 minutes

Servings: 2

Ingredients:

1½ tablespoons butter, divided

1 large sweet potatoes, peeled and spiralized with Blade C

Salt and freshly ground black pepper, to taste

1 egg

¼ cup peanut butter

½ small banana, peeled and sliced

4 fresh strawberries, hulled and sliced

1 teaspoon honey

Directions:

1. In a large skillet, melt ½ tablespoon of butter on medium heat.
2. Add sweet potato noodles and sprinkle with salt and black pepper and cook for about 6-8 minutes.
3. Transfer the sweet potato noodles into a bowl.
4. Add egg and mix well.
5. Transfer the mixture into 2 (6-ounce) ramekins, half way full. Cover the ramekins with wax paper.
6. Now, place a weight over noodles to press firmly down.
7. Refrigerate for at least 15-20 minutes.

8. In a large skillet, melt remaining butter on medium-low heat.

9. Carefully, transfer the sweet potato patties into skillet and cook for about 3-4 minutes.

10. Flip the side and cook for about 2-3 minutes more.

11. Place patties in serving plate.

12. Spread peanut butter over patties evenly. T

13. Top with banana slices and strawberries.

14. Drizzle with honey and serve.

Butter Sweet Potato Buns Sandwich

Time: 45 minutes

Servings: 2

Ingredients:

3 tablespoons olive oil, divided

1 garlic clove, minced

2 medium sweet potatoes, peeled and spiralized with Blade C

Salt and freshly ground black pepper, to taste

2 eggs, beaten

1 medium onion, sliced into rings

1 medium avocado, peeled, pitted and sliced

3 tablespoons butter, softened

4 tomato slices

8 fresh baby spinach leaves

Directions:

1. In a large skillet, heat 1 tablespoon of oil on medium heat.
2. Add garlic and sauté for about 1 minute.
3. Add sweet potato noodles and sprinkle with salt and black pepper and cook for about 6-8 minutes.
4. Transfer the sweet potato mixture into a bowl.
5. Add beaten eggs and mix well.
6. Transfer the mixture into 4 ramekins, half way full.
7. Cover the ramekins with wax paper.
8. Now, place a weight over noodles to press firmly down.
9. Refrigerate for at least 20 minutes.
10. Meanwhile in a skillet, heat ¼ tablespoon of oil on medium heat.
11. Add onion and sprinkle with salt and black pepper and sauté for about 4-5 minutes.
12. Transfer the onion into a plate and keep aside.
13. In the same skillet, add tomato slices and sear for about 1 minute per side.
14. Transfer the tomato slices into a plate and keep aside.
15. In a bowl, add avocado and butter and with a fork, mash till well combined.
15. In a large skillet, heat remaining oil on medium-low heat.

16. Carefully, transfer the sweet potato bun into skillet and cook for about 3-4 minutes.

17. Flip the side and cook for about 2-3 minutes more.

18. In a serving plate place 1 bun.

19. Spread avocado mixture over all buns.

20. Place spinach leaves over buns and top with onion rings and tomato slices evenly.

21. Cover with other bun.

22. Repeat with remaining buns.

23. Secure with a toothpick before serving.

Chicken Zucchini Buns Sandwich

Time: 25 minutes

Servings: 2

Ingredients:

For Buns:

2 tablespoons olive oil, divided

2 garlic cloves, minced

3 large zucchinis, spiralized with Blade C

Salt and freshly ground black pepper, to taste

2 large eggs, beaten

2 egg whites, beaten

For Avocado Mash:

1 avocado, peeled, pitted and chopped

1½ tablespoons fresh parsley leaves, minced

Pinch of salt

Pinch of red pepper flakes, crushed

For Sandwiches:

2 red onion slices

2 large tomato slices

4-ounce cooked chicken breast, chopped

2 romaine lettuce leaves, torn

Directions:

1. In a large skillet, heat 1 tablespoon of oil on medium heat.
2. Add garlic and sauté for about 1 minute.
3. Add zucchini and sprinkle with salt and black pepper and cook for about 3-4 minutes.
4. Transfer the zucchini mixture into a bowl.
5. Immediately, add beaten eggs and egg whites and mix well.
6. Transfer the mixture into 2 large ramekins, half way full.
7. Cover the ramekins with wax paper.
8. Now, place a weight over wax paper to press firmly down.
9. Refrigerate for at least 20 minutes.
10. In a large skillet, heat remaining oil on medium-low heat.
11. Carefully, transfer the zucchini bun into skillet and cook for about 2-3 minutes per side.

12. Transfer the buns into a plate.
13. Meanwhile in a bowl, add all mash ingredients and with a fork, mash till smooth and creamy.
14. Preheat the grill to medium heat.
15. Grease the grill grate.
16. Grill onion slices for 2 minutes, flipping once after 1 minute.
17. Grill the tomato slices for 1 minute, flipping once after 30 seconds.
18. In a serving plate place 1 bun.
19. Spread avocado mash over buns evenly.
20. Place 1 onion slices over mash, followed by half of chicken, 1 tomato slice and half of torn lettuce.
21. Cover with other bun.
22. Repeat with remaining buns.
23. Secure with a toothpick before serving.

Yummy Zucchini Patties & Sweet Potato

Time: 60 minutes

Servings: 4

Ingredients:

1 large egg

¼ teaspoon ground cumin

½ teaspoon red pepper flakes, crushed

Salt and freshly ground black pepper, to taste

¼ cup butter, melted

2 tablespoons almond flour

1 large zucchini, spiralized with Blade C and chopped1 large sweet potato, peeled, spiralized with Blade C and chopped

2 tablespoons fresh cilantro leaves, chopped

Directions:

1. Preheat the oven to 375 degrees F.
2. Line 2 baking sheets with greased parchment papers.
3. In a large bowl, add egg and spices and beat well.
4. Add butter and flour and mix till well combined.
5. Add remaining ingredients and mix till well combined.
6. With ½ cup of mixture make a patty.
7. Repeat with the remaining mixture.
8. Arrange the patties onto prepared baking sheets in a single layer.
1. Bake for about 10 minutes.
2. Reduce the temperature of oven to 350 degrees F.
3. Bake for about 15 minutes.
4. Carefully, flip the side of patties and bake for about 15 minutes.

Almond Cumin Carrot & Zucchini Patties

Time: 25 minutes

Servings: 4

Ingredients:

1 medium zucchini, spiralized with Blade C

1 medium carrot, peeled and spiralized with Blade C

4-5 scallions, chopped

2 small eggs, beaten

½ cup almond flour

¼ teaspoon ground cumin

¼ teaspoon red pepper flakes, crushed

1 teaspoon ground turmeric

Salt and freshly ground black pepper, to taste

2 tablespoons extra virgin olive oil

Directions:

1. In a large bowl, add all ingredients except oil and mix till well combined.

2. In a large skillet, heat ½ tablespoon of oil on medium-high heat.

3. Place ¼ of the mixture in oil and gently press down like a patty.

4. Cook for about 5-6 minutes, flipping once after 3 minutes.

5. Repeat with the remaining oil and veggie mixture.

Delight Spinach Sweet Potato Muffins

Time: 50 minutes

Servings: 3

Ingredients:

1½ tablespoons olive oil, divided

1 garlic clove, minced

1 large sweet potato, peeled and spiralized with Blade C

Salt and freshly ground black pepper, to taste

3 cups fresh spinach, torn

12 egg whites, beaten lightly

Directions:

1. Preheat the oven to 375 degrees F.

2. Grease a 6 cups of a muffin tin.

3. In a large skillet, heat oil on medium heat.

4. Add garlic and sauté for about 1 minute.

5. Add sweet potato noodles and sprinkle with salt and black pepper and cook for about 6-8 minutes.

6. Transfer the sweet potato mixture into a plate and keep aside.

7. In the same skillet, add spinach and cook for about 3-4 minutes.

8. Add egg whites in prepared muffin cups, about ½-inch full.

9. Place sweet potato noodles over egg whites, followed by spinach and remaining egg whites evenly.

10. Bake for about 20 minutes.

Cilantro Carrot & Zucchini Loaf

Time: 75 minutes

Servings: 4

Ingredients:

2 tablespoons olive oil

2 garlic cloves, minced

1 jalapeño pepper, seeded and chopped finely

4 medium zucchinis, spiralized with Blade C and chopped

4 medium carrots, peeled, spiralized with Blade C and chopped

¼ teaspoon red pepper flakes, crushed

Salt and freshly ground black pepper, to taste

¼ cup coconut flour

½ teaspoon baking powder

6 large eggs

¼ cup unsweetened coconut milk

2 tablespoons fresh cilantro leaves, chopped

Directions:

1. Preheat the oven to 350 degrees F.

2. Line a loaf pan with parchment paper.

3. In a skillet, heat oil on medium heat.

4. Add garlic and jalapeño pepper and sauté for about 1 minute.

5. Add zucchini, carrot, red pepper flakes, salt and black pepper and cook for about 8-9 minutes.

6. Remove from heat and keep aside to cool.

7. In a bowl, mix together flour, baking powder and pinch of salt.

8. In another bowl, add eggs and coconut milk and beat till well combined.

9. Mix egg mixture into flour mixture.

10. Fold in zucchini mixture and cilantro.

11. Transfer the mixture into prepared loaf pan evenly.

12. Bake for about 40-45 minutes or till a toothpick inserted in the center comes out clean.

Pumpkin Spice Sweet Potato Waffles

Time: 25 minutes

Servings: 2

Ingredients:

1 tablespoon olive oil

2 medium sweet potatoes, peeled and spiralized with Blade C

2 teaspoons pumpkin pie spice

2 eggs, beaten

2 tablespoons pure maple syrup

Directions:

1. Preheat the waffle iron and then grease it.
2. In a large skillet, heat oil on medium heat.
3. Add sweet potato and cook for about 8-10 minutes.
4. Transfer the sweet potato mixture into a large bowl.
5. Sprinkle with pumpkin pie spice and mix well.
6. Add eggs and stir to combine.
7. Place the mixture in waffle iron and cook for about 5 minutes.
8. Serve with the drizzling of maple syrup.

Garlic Egg Parsnip Waffles

Time: 25 minutes

Servings: 2

Ingredients:

1 tablespoon olive oil

1 garlic clove, minced

4 large parsnips, peeled and spiralized with Blade C

Salt and freshly ground black pepper, to taste

1/3 cup scallions, chopped finely

2 large eggs, beaten

Directions:

1. Preheat the waffle iron and then grease it.
2. In a large skillet, heat oil on medium heat.
3. Add garlic and sauté for about 1 minute.
4. Add parsnip noodles, salt and black pepper and cook for about 4-5 minutes.
5. Transfer the parsnip mixture into a large bowl.
6. Add scallions and eggs and stir to combine.
7. Pour the mixture in waffle iron and cook for about 5 minutes.

Cheddar Potato Pancakes

Time: 30 minutes

Servings: 4

Ingredients:

2 tablespoons olive oil, divided

1 garlic clove, minced

1 tablespoon fresh rosemary, chopped

¼ teaspoon red pepper flakes, crushed

4 medium potatoes, peeled and spiralized with Blade C

Salt and freshly ground black pepper, to taste

4 eggs, beaten

1 cup cheddar cheese, grated

Directions:

1. In a large skillet, heat one tablespoon of oil on medium heat.
2. Add garlic, rosemary and red pepper flakes and sauté for about 1 minute.
3. Stir in potatoes, salt and black pepper and cook, covered for about 8-10 minutes.
4. Transfer the potato mixture into a large bowl.
5. Add eggs and cheese and stir to combine.
6. In another large skillet, heat remaining oil on medium heat.
7. Add 1 cup of potato mixture and flatten with the back of a spoon.
8. Cook for about 2-3 minutes per side.
9. Repeat with the remaining mixture.
10. Serve immediately.

Honey Zucchini Pancakes

Time: 25 minutes

Servings: 4

Ingredients:

½ cup almond flour

1 tablespoon flax meal

1/3 teaspoon baking soda

Pinch of salt

1 egg, separated

½ tablespoon honey

1 tablespoon coconut oil, melted

½ cup unsweetened almond milk

½ cup zucchini, spiralized with Blade C and chopped

Directions:

1. Preheat a greased griddle.

2. In a large bowl, mix together flour, flax meal, baking soda and salt.

3. In another bowl, add egg yolk, honey, oil and milk and beat till well combined.

4. Add honey mixture into flour mixture and mix well.

5. In a small bowl, add egg white and beat till soft peaks form.

6. Fold egg white into flour mixture.

7. Now fold in zucchini.

8. Place ¼ cup of mixture into griddle and cook for about 1-2 minutes per side.

9. Repeat with remaining mixture.

Avocado Sweet Potato & Chicken Rolls

Time: 30 minutes

Servings: 2

Ingredients:

1 medium ripe avocado, peeled, pitted and mashed

1½ tablespoons olive oil, divided

1 large sweet potato, peeled and spiralized with Blade C

4 eggs, beaten

Salt and freshly ground black pepper, to taste

2 large lettuce leaves, pat dried

¼ cup grilled chicken, shredded

Directions:

1. In a large skillet, heat 1 tablespoon of oil on medium heat.

2. Add sweet potato noodles and cook for about 6-8 minutes.

3. Transfer the sweet potato noodles into a plate.

4. In the same skillet, heat remaining oil on medium heat.

5. Add eggs and sprinkle with salt and black pepper and cook for about 2-3 minutes or till eggs are done completely.

6. Remove from heat.

7. Arrange the both lettuce leaves in 2 serving plates.

8. Place mashed avocado over both leaves evenly and top with sweet potato noodles, followed by scrambled eggs and shredded chicken.

9. Carefully roll the lettuce leaves and serve.

Tapioca Zucchini & Chicken Pizza

Time: 50 minutes

Servings: 4

Ingredients:

For Crust:

1½ cups almond meal

1 cup coconut flour

1 cup tapioca flour

1½ teaspoons baking powder

Pinch of sea salt

5 eggs

5 tablespoons olive oil

1 cup water

2 garlic cloves, minced

1 tablespoon fresh rosemary, minced

For Tomato Sauce:

2 cups fresh tomatoes, chopped

1 tablespoon fresh basil leaves, chopped

1 tablespoon olive oil

1 tablespoon fresh lemon juice

Salt and freshly ground black pepper, to taste

For Topping:

1 cup cooked chicken, cubed

1 medium zucchini, spiralized with Blade C and chopped

8-10 black olives, pitted and sliced

Pinch of red pepper flakes, crushed

Pinch of salt

Directions:

1. Preheat the oven to 350 degrees F.

2. Grease a pizza pan and then line with a parchment paper.

3. For crust in a bowl, mix together almond meal, flours, baking powder and salt.

4. In another bowl, add eggs, oil and water and beat till well combined.

5. Mix egg mixture into flour mixture.

6. Fold in garlic and rosemary and mix till a dough form.

7. Place the dough into prepared pan evenly.

8. Bake for about 15 minutes.

9. Remove from oven and keep aside to cool slightly.

10. Carefully remove parchment paper from underneath the crust.

11. Meanwhile for tomato sauce in a blender, add all ingredients and pulse till smooth.

12. Spread tomato sauce over crust evenly.

13. Place chicken and zucchini over tomato sauce and top with olives.

14. Sprinkle with red pepper flakes and salt.

15. Bake for about 10-12 minutes.

Scallion Zucchini & Egg Bake

Time: 70 minutes

Servings: 4

Ingredients:

4 large eggs

2 tablespoons heavy cream

1 tablespoon coconut oil, melted

¼ cup almond meal, divided

Salt and freshly ground black pepper, to taste

4 cups zucchini, spiralized with Blade C

1 scallion, sliced thinly

Directions:

1. Preheat the oven to 300 degrees F.

2. Grease an 8x8-inch baking dish.

3. In a large bowl, add eggs, cream, oil, 3 tablespoons of almond meal, salt and black pepper and beat till well combined.

4. Stir in zucchini.

5. Place 1/3 of zucchini noodles into prepared baking dish and top with 1/3 of scallion.

6. Repeat the layers twice.

7. Pour the any remaining egg mixture from bowl over the layers.

8. Sprinkle with remaining almond meal evenly.

9. Bake for about 50 minutes or till done completely.

Garlic Spicy Zucchini Chicken

Time: 40 minutes

Servings: 4

Ingredients:

2 tablespoons olive oil, divided

1½ pound skinless, boneless chicken breast, trimmed and cubed

½ teaspoon ground cumin

Salt and freshly ground black pepper, to taste

2 garlic cloves, minced

2 jalapeño pepper, seeded and minced

3 large zucchinis, spiralized with Blade C

½ cup fresh cilantro, chopped

Directions:

1. In a large skillet, heat 1 tablespoon of oil on medium heat.
2. Add chicken, cumin, salt and black pepper and cook for about 5-7 minutes.
3. Transfer the chicken into a bowl.
4. In the same skillet, heat remaining oil on medium heat.
5. Add garlic and jalapeño pepper and sauté for about 1 minute.
6. Add zucchini noodles, salt and black pepper and cook for about 2-3 minutes.
7. Stir in chicken and cilantro and coo k for about 2 minutes.
8. Serve hot.

Tamari Zucchini with Chicken

Time: 30 minutes

Servings: 4

Ingredients:

1 tablespoon coconut oil

3 garlic cloves, minced

1 pound boneless chicken thighs, cut into thin strips

1 tablespoon tamari

½ tablespoon fresh lime juice

½ tablespoon balsamic vinegar

½ tablespoon honey

2 large zucchinis, spiralized with Blade C

Salt and freshly ground black pepper, to taste

¼ cup fresh parsley leaves, chopped

1 tablespoon black sesame seeds, toasted

Directions:

1. In a large skillet, melt coconut oil on medium heat.
2. Add garlic and sauté for about 1 minute.
3. Add chicken and stir fry for about 3-4 minutes.
4. Add tamari, lime juice, vinegar and honey and cook for about 4-5 minutes.
5. Stir in zucchini, salt and black pepper and cook for about 3-4 minutes.
6. Stir in parsley and immediately remove from heat.
7. Garnish with sesame seeds and serve hot.

Eggplant Zucchini & Chicken

Time: 40 minutes

Servings: 2

Ingredients:

1½ cups eggplant, diced into ¾-inch pieces

2 tablespoons olive oil, divided

Salt and freshly ground black pepper, to taste

3 small garlic cloves, minced

½ pound skinless boneless chicken, cut into bite size pieces

1½ cups fresh tomatoes, chopped finely

2 medium zucchinis, spiralized with Blade C

2 tablespoons fresh basil, chopped

Directions:

1. Preheat the oven to 475 degrees F.
2. Line a baking sheet with parchment paper.
3. Arrange eggplant pieces in prepared baking sheet in a single layer.

4. Drizzle with 1 tablespoon of oil and sprinkle with salt and black pepper.

5. Roast for about 25 minutes, flipping occasionally.

6. Meanwhile in a large skillet, heat remaining oil on medium heat.

7. Add garlic and sauté for about 1 minute.

8. Add chicken and cook for about 8-10 minutes.

9. Add tomatoes and cook for about 8-10 minutes.

10. Stir in zucchini, basil and seasoning and cook for about 3-4 minutes.

11. Stir in roasted eggplant and serve hot.

Chili Chicken With Broccoli & Zucchini

Time: 35 minutes

Servings: 2

Ingredients:

2 tablespoons olive oil

1 large garlic clove, minced

2 (6-ounce) skinless, boneless chicken breasts, cubed

¼ teaspoon red chili powder

Salt and freshly ground black pepper, to taste

1 broccoli head, cut into florets

¾ cup chicken broth

2 large zucchinis, spiralized with Blade C

1 tablespoon fresh parsley, chopped

Directions:

1. In a large skillet, heat oil on medium heat.
2. Add garlic and sauté for about 1 minute.
3. Add chicken and sprinkle with chili powder, salt and black pepper and cook for about 6-8 minutes or till golden brown from all sides.
4. Add broccoli and cook for 2-3 minutes.
5. Add broth and cook for about 2-3 minutes.
6. Stir in zucchini noodles and parsley and cook for about 2-3 minutes.
7. Serve hot.

Garlic Chicken Zucchini & Kale

Time: 45 minutes

Servings: 2

Ingredients:

2 (4-ounce) skinless, boneless chicken breasts, sliced into thin strips

1½ tablespoons fresh lemon juice, divided

2 teaspoons dried rosemary, crushed

½ teaspoon cayenne pepper, divided

Salt and freshly ground black pepper, to taste

1 tablespoon olive oil, divided

1 garlic clove, minced

2 cups fresh kale, trimmed and chopped

2 large zucchinis, spiralized with Blade C

1 teaspoon fresh lemon zest, grated finely

Directions:

1. Preheat the oven to 350 degrees F.
2. Grease a baking dish.
3. Place chicken strips in prepared baking dish.
4. Drizzle with 1 tablespoon of lemon juice and sprinkle with rosemary, ¼ teaspoon of cayenne pepper, salt and black pepper.
5. Bake for about 15-20 minutes.
6. Remove from oven and keep aside.
7. Meanwhile in a large skillet, heat oil on medium heat.
8. Add garlic and sauté for about 1 minute.
9. Add kale and cook for about 3 minutes.
10. Stir in zucchini noodles, remaining cayenne pepper and lemon juice and cook for about 2-3 minutes, stirring occasionally.
11. Stir in chicken and immediately, remove from heat.
12. Garnish with lemon zest and serve hot.

Tomatoes Zucchini & Chicken

Time: 45 minutes

Servings: 2

Ingredients:

2 cups grape tomatoes

1 tablespoon olive oil

Salt and freshly ground black pepper, to taste

2 garlic cloves, minced

2 cups mixed fresh greens (kale, spinach, arugula), torn

2 large zucchinis, spiralized with Blade C

1 cup cooked skinless, boneless chicken breast, cubed

Directions:

1. Preheat the oven to 400 degrees F.
2. Arrange the grape tomatoes in a baking dish.
3. Drizzle with oil evenly and sprinkle with salt and black pepper.
4. Roast for about 20 minutes.
5. Remove from oven and keep aside.
6. Meanwhile in a large skillet, heat oil on medium heat.
7. Add garlic and sauté for about 1 minute.
8. Add greens and cook for about 2-3 minutes.
9. Add zucchini noodles, chicken and roasted tomatoes and cook for about 2-3 minutes, stirring occasionally.
10. Serve hot.

Chicken Zucchini & Radish

Time: 25 minutes

Servings: 2

Ingredients:

For Zucchini & Radish:

2 tablespoons olive oil

5 radishes, peeled and spiralized with Blade C

1 large zucchini, spiralized with Blade C

Salt and freshly ground black pepper, to taste

1 cup grilled skinless, boneless chicken thighs, cubed

For Pesto:

2 cups fresh baby spinach

½ cup fresh basil, chopped

1 garlic clove, minced

½ cup pecans, chopped and divided

1 tablespoon fresh lemon juice

½ cup water

Salt and freshly ground black pepper, to taste

Directions:

1. In a large skillet, heat oil on medium heat.
2. Add radish and zucchini noodles and cook for about 2-3 minutes.
3. Stir in salt and black pepper and remove from heat.
4. Transfer the noodles into a large bowl.
5. In a food processor, add spinach, basil, garlic, ½ cup of pecans, lemon juice, water, salt and black pepper and pulse till smooth.
6. Place the pesto mixture over vegetables and gently toss to coat.
7. Top with grilled chicken and serve.

Zucchini with Spinach & Chicken

Time: 35 minutes

Servings: 2

Ingredients:

1 (6-ounce) skinless, boneless chicken breast, sliced into thin strips

1 tablespoon fresh rosemary, minced

Salt and freshly ground black pepper, to taste

1 tablespoon olive oil

1 garlic clove, minced

2 cups fresh spinach, chopped

2 medium zucchinis, spiralized with Blade C

½ tablespoon fresh lime juice

Directions:

1. Preheat the oven to 350 degrees F.
2. Grease a baking dish.
3. Arrange the chicken strips into prepared baking dish.
4. Sprinkle with rosemary, salt and black pepper.
5. Bake for about 15-20 minutes.
6. Remove from oven and keep aside.
7. Meanwhile in a skillet, heat oil on medium heat.
8. Add garlic and sauté for about 1 minute.
9. Add spinach and cook for about 2-3 minutes.
10. Add zucchini, salt and black pepper and cook for about 34 minutes.
11. Stir in chicken and lime juice and remove from heat.
12. Serve hot.

Black Pepper Zucchini with Spinach & Chicken

Time: 25 minutes

Servings: 2

Ingredients:

1 tablespoons olive oil

2 garlic cloves, minced

2 skinless, boneless chicken breasts, trimmed and cut into thin strips

Salt and freshly ground black pepper, to taste

2 large zucchinis, spiralized with Blade C

2 cups fresh spinach, chopped

¼ cup feta cheese, crumbled

Directions:

1. In a large skillet, heat oil on medium heat.

2. Add garlic and sauté for about 1 minute.

3. Add chicken and sprinkle with salt and black pepper and stir fry for about 6-8 minutes or till browned from all sides.

4. Add zucchini and spinach and cook for about 3-4 minutes.

5. Stir in salt and black pepper and remove from heat.

6. Top with feta cheese and serve.

Chicken Bake With Zucchini, Mushrooms

Time: 65 minutes

Servings: 4

Ingredients:

¼ cup coconut oil, divided

1½ pound boneless chicken breasts, cut into thin strips

Salt and freshly ground black pepper, to taste

½ cup white onion, chopped

2 cups fresh mushrooms, sliced

3 garlic cloves, minced

1 tablespoon fresh rosemary, chopped

½ cup coconut cream

½ cup chicken broth

2 tablespoons fresh lemon juice

6 medium zucchinis, spiralized with Blade C

1 cup almond meal

¼ cup fresh basil leave, chopped

2 tablespoons almonds, chopped

Directions:

1. Preheat the oven to 375 degrees F.

2. Lightly, grease a casserole dish.

3. In a large skillet, melt 2 tablespoons of coconut oil on medium heat.

4. Add chicken and sprinkle with salt and black pepper and cook for about 4-5 minutes.

5. Transfer the chicken into a plate.

6. Now, add onion and mushroom and sauté for about 3-4 minutes.

7. Add garlic and rosemary and sauté for about 1 minute.

8. Add coconut cream, broth and lemon juice and bring to a boil.

9. Reduce the heat to medium-low and simmer for about 5 minutes or till sauce becomes thick.

10. Remove from heat and stir in chicken, zucchinis, salt and black pepper.

11. Transfer the mixture into prepared casserole dish.

12. In a bowl, add almond meal, remaining oil and some salt and with your hands mix till crumbly.

13. Spread the crumbly mixture over zucchini mixture evenly.

14. Bake for about 25-30 minutes.

15. Garnish with basil and chopped almonds before serving.

Chicken With Kale &Yellow Squash

Time: 30 minutes

Servings: 2

Ingredients:

1½ tablespoons olive oil

1 garlic clove, minced

2 (6-ounce) skinless, boneless chicken breasts, cubed

Salt and freshly ground black pepper, to taste

2 cups fresh kale, trimmed and chopped

2 large yellow squash, spiralized with Blade C

1 tablespoon fresh lime juice

Directions:

1. In a large skillet, heat oil on medium heat.

2. Add garlic and sauté for about 1 minute.

3. Add chicken and sprinkle with salt and black pepper and cook for about 6-8 minutes or till golden brown from all sides.

4. Add kale and cook for about 2-3 minutes.

5. Stir in squash noodles and lime juice and cook for about 23 minutes.

6. Serve hot.

Chicken With Yellow Squash & Tomatoes

Time: 65 minutes

Servings: 4

Ingredients:

4-6 medium yellow squash, spiralized with Blade C

3 tablespoons olive oil, divided

Salt and freshly ground black pepper, to taste

1 pound skinless, boneless chicken breasts, cut into thin strips

1 white onion, chopped

3-4 garlic cloves, minced

¾ pound grape tomatoes, halved

1¼ cups chicken broth

½ cup fresh baby spinach

1 tablespoon fresh oregano

1 tablespoon fresh thyme, chopped

Directions:

1. Preheat the oven to 400 degrees F.
2. Grease a large baking sheet.
3. Place squash noodles into prepared baking sheet.
4. Drizzle with 1 tablespoon of oil and sprinkle with salt and black pepper.
5. Bake for about 25 minutes, tossing once after 10 minutes.
6. Remove from oven and toss the squash.
7. Bake for 15 minutes more. Remove from oven and keep aside.

8. In a large skillet, heat 1 tablespoon of oil on medium heat.

9. Add chicken and sprinkle with salt and black pepper and cook for about 8-10 minutes or till golden brown from all sides.

10. Transfer the chicken into a plate.

11. In the same skillet, heat remaining oil on medium heat.

12. Add onion and sauté for about 3-4 minutes.

13. Add garlic and sauté for about 1 minute.

14. Add tomatoes and broth and cook for about 2-3 minutes.

15. Add chicken, squash, spinach and herbs and cook for about 2 minutes.

16. Serve hot.

Pumpkin Puree Chicken With Yellow Squash

Time: 40 minutes

Servings: 4

Ingredients:

2 tablespoons extra virgin olive oil

1 small white onion, chopped

2 garlic cloves, minced

2 cups canned pumpkin puree

½ cup coconut milk

2 cups chicken broth

2 tablespoons fresh basil leaves, chopped and divided

Salt and freshly ground black pepper, to taste

4 large yellow squash, spiralized with Blade C

1 pound grilled skinless, boneless chicken breast, cubed

Directions:

1. In a large skillet, heat oil on medium-low heat.
2. Add onion and sauté for about 3-4 minutes.
3. Add garlic and sauté for 1 minute.
4. Stir in pumpkin, coconut milk, broth, 1 tablespoon of basil and seasoning.
5. Reduce the heat to low and simmer for about 10 minutes, stirring occasionally.
6. Stir in squash noodles and chicken and cook for about 4-5 minutes.
7. Top with remaining basil and serve hot.

Tasty Sweet Potato with Asparagus & Chicken

Time: 35 minutes

Servings: 4

Ingredients:

2 tablespoons olive oil

1 large garlic clove, minced

2 (4-ounce) skinless, boneless chicken breasts, cubed

Salt and freshly ground black pepper, to taste

1 large sweet potatoes, peeled and spiralized with Blade C

½ cup chicken broth

8 asparagus stalks, trimmed and cut into 2-inch pieces

2 tablespoons fresh basil, chopped

½ tablespoon fresh lemon juice

Directions:

1. In a large skillet, heat oil on medium heat.
2. Add garlic and sauté for about 1 minute.
3. Add chicken and sprinkle with salt and black pepper and cook for about 6 to 8 minutes or till golden brown from all sides.
4. Add sweet potato noodles and broth and cook for about 2-3 minutes.
5. Stir in asparagus and basil and cook for about 4-5 minutes.
6. Drizzle with lemon juice and serve hot.

Scallion Chicken Sweet Potato

Time: 50 minutes

Servings: 4

Ingredients:

For Sauce:

4½ cups cauliflower, chopped

1 small garlic clove, minced

1½ cups coconut milk

½ cup chicken broth

Salt, to taste

For Scallions:

1 tablespoon olive oil

4 cups scallions, sliced

1 tablespoon fresh lime juice

2 tablespoons chicken broth

For Chicken & Sweet Potato:

2 large sweet potatoes, peeled and spiralized with Blade C

2 cups grilled skinless, boneless chicken breast, cubed

Salt and freshly ground black pepper, to taste

1 teaspoon lime zest, grated freshly

3 tablespoons fresh cilantro Leaves, chopped

Directions:

1. For sauce in a pan of boiling water, add cauliflower and cook for about 10 minutes.

2. Drain well and keep aside to cool slightly.

3. In a food processor, add cauliflower and remaining ingredients and pulse till creamy and smooth.

4. Transfer into a large bowl and keep aside.

5. In a large skillet, heat oil on low heat.

6. Add scallions and cook for about 15 minutes.

7. Stir in lime juice, broth and salt and cook for about 5 minutes more.

8. Remove from heat and add into bowl with creamy sauce.

9. In another pan of boiling water, add sweet potato noodles and cook for about 4-5 minutes.

10. Drain well.

11. In a large skillet, add scallion mixture, sweet potato and chicken and cook for about 2-3 minutes or till heated completely. S

12. Season with salt and black pepper and remove from heat.

13. Top with lime zest and cilantro and serve immediately.

Ginger Chicken With Veggies & Sweet Potato

Time: 40 minutes

Servings: 4

Ingredients:

1 tablespoon olive oil

½ teaspoon fresh ginger, minced

1 teaspoon garlic, minced

½ teaspoon cayenne pepper

1 large red bell pepper, seeded and sliced thinly

1 large green bell pepper, seeded and sliced thinly

1 cup cauliflower, cut into small florets

½ cup vegetable broth

1¾ cups coconut milk

3 sweet potatoes, peeled and spiralized with Blade C

Salt and freshly ground black pepper, to taste

2 tablespoons fresh parsley, chopped

Directions:

1. In a large skillet, heat oil on medium heat.
2. Add ginger, garlic and cayenne pepper and sauté for about 30 seconds.
3. Add bell peppers and cauliflower and cook for about 1-2 minutes.
4. Add broth and bring to a boil.
5. Reduce the heat to medium-low and simmer for about 4-5 minutes.
6. Stir in coconut milk and sweet potato and simmer for about 6-8 minutes.
7. Garnish with parsley and serve.

Rosemary Artichokes & Chicken With Sweet Potato

Time: 50 minutes

Servings: 2

Ingredients:

1½ cups artichoke hearts, quartered

2 tablespoons olive oil, divided

Salt and freshly ground black pepper, to taste

1 skinless, boneless chicken breast, trimmed

½ teaspoon dried rosemary, crushed

¼ cup white onion, chopped

2 garlic cloves, minced

¼ teaspoon dried oregano, crushed

¼ teaspoon red pepper flakes, crushed

2 cups fresh tomatoes, chopped finely

¼ cup vegetable broth

1 large sweet potato, spiralized with Blade C

1 tablespoon fresh cilantro leaves, chopped

Directions:

1. Preheat the oven to 375 degrees F.
2. Lightly, grease 2 large baking dishes.
3. In a large bowl, add artichoke hearts, ½ tablespoon of oil, salt and black pepper and toss to coat well.
4. Transfer the artichoke mixture into a prepared baking dish.
5. In another bowl, add chicken breast, rosemary, ½ tablespoon of oil, salt and black pepper and toss to coat well.
6. Transfer the chicken mixture into another prepared baking dish.
7. Bake artichoke for about 10 minutes.
8. Now, place the baking dish of chicken in oven.
9. Bake chicken and artichoke for about 20 minutes.
10. Remove from oven and keep aside to cool slightly.
11. Cut chicken into bite sized pieces.
12. Meanwhile in a skillet, heat remaining oil on medium heat.
13. Add onion and sauté for about 3-4 minutes.
14. Add garlic, oregano and red pepper flakes and sauté for about 1 minute.
15. Add tomatoes and broth and cook for about 2 minutes.

16. Stir in sweet potato, salt and black pepper and cook, covered for about 3 minutes.
17. Uncover and cook for about 4-5 minutes.
18. Stir in cooked chicken and artichoke and remove from heat.
19. Garnish with cilantro and serve.

Brussels Sprout Chicken & Sweet Potato

Time: 40 minutes

Servings: 2

Ingredients:

1 cup Brussels sprouts, halved

Salt, to taste

2 tablespoons extra virgin olive oil, divided

2 medium sweet potatoes, peeled and spiralized with Blade C

1 garlic clove, minced

½ pound skinless, boneless chicken breast, cut into bite sized pieces

2 cups fresh spinach, torn

1 cup chicken broth

Freshly ground black pepper, to taste

Directions:

1. Preheat the oven to 375 degrees F.
2. Lightly, grease a large baking dish.
3. Arrange Brussels sprouts in prepared baking dish and sprinkle with salt.
4. Roast for about 25 minutes.
5. Meanwhile in a large skillet, heat 1 tablespoon of oil on medium heat.
6. Add sweet potato noodles and cook for about 8-10 minutes.
7. Transfer the sweet potato into a bowl and keep aside.
8. In the same skillet, heat remaining oil on medium heat.
9. Add garlic and sauté for about 1 minute.
10. Add chicken and cook for about 10 minutes.
11. Add spinach and cook for about 1 minute.
12. Add broth and bring to a boil on high heat.
13. Reduce the heat to medium-low and simmer for about 4-5 minutes.
14. Stir in Brussels sprouts and sweet potatoes and cook for about 2-3 minutes.
15. Season with salt and black pepper and serve.

Chicken Curry & Sweet Potato

Time: 30 minutes

Servings: 4

Ingredients:

For Chicken:

1 tablespoon olive oil

1 pound skinless, boneless chicken breast, trimmed and cubed

1 tablespoon curry powder

½ teaspoon cayenne pepper

¼ cup white onion, chopped

1 cup red bell pepper, seeded and chopped

1 cup coconut milk

½ cup chicken broth

½ cup coconut cream

Salt and freshly ground black pepper, to taste

¼ cup cashews, chopped

For Sweet Potato:

1 tablespoon olive oil

1 teaspoon curry powder

2 Medium sweet potato, peeled and spiralized with Blade C

¼ cup chicken broth

Directions:

1. For chicken in a large skillet, heat oil on medium heat.
2. Add chicken and stir fry for about 5-6 minutes.
3. Add curry powder and cayenne pepper and stir fry for about 1 minute.
4. Add onion and bell pepper and cook for about 3-4 minutes.
5. Add coconut milk, broth and cream and bring to a boil on high heat.
6. Reduce the heat to medium-low and simmer for about 1-2 minutes.
7. Stir in cashews, salt and black pepper and remove from heat.
8. Meanwhile for sweet potato in another large skillet, heat oil on medium heat.
9. Add sweet potato and curry powder and cook for about 1 minute.
10. Add broth and cook for about 6-7 minutes.
11. Transfer the sweet potato mixture in serving plates and top with chicken and serve.

Chicken Casserole Black Beans & Sweet Potato

Time: 1 hour 50 minutes

Servings: 6

Ingredients:

4 medium vine tomatoes

4 dried guajillo chili peppers

1 pound skinless, boneless chicken breast

1 teaspoon olive oil

1 onion, quartered

4 garlic cloves

½ teaspoon ground cumin

Salt and freshly ground black pepper, to taste

1 (15-ounce) can black beans, rinsed and drained

1 cup frozen corn

2 sweet potatoes, peeled, spiralized with Blade C and cut into 6-inch lengths

5-ounce pepper jack cheese, shredded

3 scallions chopped

Directions:

1. In a large pan of boiling water, add tomatoes and peppers and again bring to a boil.

2. Boil the tomatoes for about 10 minutes.

3. With a slotted spoon, transfer the tomatoes into a plate and keep aside to cool.

4. Then peel the skin of tomatoes.

5. Boil the peppers for about 20 minutes.

6. Drain the peppers well and keep aside to cool.

7. Cut the stem and remove the seeds and the inside of peppers.

8. Meanwhile in another large pan of boiling water, add chicken breasts and cook for about 10 minutes.

9. Drain well and keep aside to cool.

10. Shred the chicken and transfer into a large bowl.

11. Preheat oven to 400 degrees F.

12. In a medium skillet, heat oil on medium-high heat.

13. Add onion and sauté for about 4-5 minutes.

14. Add garlic, cumin, salt and black pepper and sauté for about 1 minute.

15. In a blender, add tomatoes, peppers and onion mixture and pulse till smooth.

16. Add the pureed mixture into the bowl of chicken with beans and corn and mix well.

17. Arrange the sweet potatoes noodles into a 13x9-inch casserole dish.

18. Place the chicken mixture over sweet potatoes noodles and gently, stir to combine.

19. Sprinkle cheese over the noodles mixture evenly.

20. With a piece of foil, cover the casserole dish and bake for about 1 hour.

21. Top with scallions and serve.

Parsnip & Sweet Potato Chicken Casserole

Time: 1 hour 20 minutes

Servings: 4

Ingredients:

2 sweet potatoes, peeled and spiralized with Blade C

2 parsnips, peeled and spiralized with Blade C

2 tablespoon olive oil, divided

Salt and freshly ground black pepper, to taste

2 bone-in, skin-on chicken legs

¼ cup teriyaki sauce

2 teaspoons Worcestershire sauce

2 teaspoons low-sodium soy sauce

Directions:

1. Preheat the oven to 400 degrees.

2. In a bowl, add vegetable noodles, 1 tablespoon of oil, salt and pepper and toss to coat well.

3. In a large baking dish, place the vegetable noodles and top with the chicken in a single layer.

4. Sprinkle with salt and pepper and drizzle with the teriyaki sauce, Worcestershire sauce and soy sauce.

5. Then with a brush, spread the sauces over the chicken pieces evenly.

6. Bake for about 45-60 minutes or till chicken is done completely

Rosemary Parsnip & Carrot with Chicken

Time: 30 minutes

Servings: 2

Ingredients:

For Chicken:

¼ cup olive oil

2 garlic cloves, minced

1 teaspoon dried rosemary, crushed

Salt and freshly ground black pepper, to taste

2 skinless, boneless chicken breast halves

For Vegetables:

½ cup chicken broth

2 large carrots, peeled and spiralized with Blade C

2 large parsnips, peeled and spiralized with Blade C

1 teaspoon dried rosemary, crushed

1 teaspoon dried thyme, crushed

1 teaspoon dried oregano, crushed

Salt and freshly ground black pepper, to taste

2 tablespoons fresh parsley, chopped

Directions:

1. Preheat the broiler of oven.
2. In a large bowl, mix together all ingredients except chicken.
3. Add chicken breasts and coat with mixture evenly.

4. Broil chicken breasts for about 15 minutes, flipping occasionally.

5. Remove the chicken from oven and keep aside to cool for about 10 minutes.

6. With a sharp knife cut chicken breasts into desired size pieces.

7. Meanwhile in a large skillet, add broth and remaining all ingredients except fresh parsley on medium heat.

8. Cook for 5-7 minutes or till desired doneness, stirring occasionally.

9. Top with broiled chicken.

10. Garnish with parsley and serve.

Garlic Parsnip with Capers & Chicken

Time: 40 minutes

Servings: 2

Ingredients:

For Chicken:

2 skinless, boneless chicken thighs

1 tablespoon olive oil

½ teaspoon cayenne pepper

Salt and freshly ground black pepper, to taste

For Parsnip:

1 tablespoon olive oil

1 garlic clove, minced

6 parsnips, peeled and spiralized with Blade C

1 tablespoon capers

2 tablespoons fresh cilantro leaves, chopped

Directions:

1. Preheat the oven to 425 degrees F.
2. Lightly, grease a baking pan.
3. Arrange chicken thighs in prepared baking dish.
4. Drizzle with oil and sprinkle with spices.
5. Bake for about 20-25 minutes.
6. Remove the thighs from oven and keep aside for about 10 minutes.
7. With a sharp knife cut into desired size pieces.
8. Meanwhile in a large skillet, heat oil on medium heat.
9. Add garlic and sauté for about 1 minute.
10. Stir in parsnip noodles.
11. Reduce the heat to low and simmer for about 15-20 minutes, stirring occasionally.
12. Stir in capers and cilantro and immediately remove from heat.
13. Top with chicken and serve.

Cheddar Thyme Broccoli with Chicken

Time: 50 minutes

Servings: 4

Ingredients:

3 tablespoons olive oil, divided

1 pound boneless chicken, diced

Salt and freshly ground black pepper, to taste

2 large broccoli heads, cut into florets and stems spiralized with Blade B

½ cup white onion, chopped

2 garlic cloves, minced

½ cup chicken broth

¼ teaspoon dried parsley, crushed

¼ teaspoon dried thyme, crushed

¼ teaspoon onion powder

1 cup sharp cheddar cheese, shredded

1/2 cup Gouda cheese, shredded

Directions:

1. *Preheat the oven to 400 degrees F.*
2. *In an oven safe skillet, heat 1 tablespoon oil on medium heat.*
3. *Add the chicken and season with salt and pepper and cook for about 3-5 or till browned completely.*
4. *Transfer the chicken in to a plate.*
5. *In the same skillet, heat the remaining oil on medium-high heat.*
6. *Add onion and garlic and cook for about 5-8 minutes.*

7. Meanwhile in a pan of salted boiling water, cook the broccoli florets and the broccoli noodles for about 2-3 minutes.

8. Drain well.

9. In the skillet, add broth and cook for about 2 minutes.

10. Stir in the chicken, broccoli florets, noodles, thyme, parsley and onion powder.

11. Remove from the heat and top with the both cheeses

12. With a piece of foil, cover the skillet and bake for about 25 minutes.

13. Remove the foil and broil for about 1-2 minutes.

Delicious Chicken Mixed Veggies

Time: 40 minutes

Servings: 4

Ingredients:

2 tablespoons butter

1 garlic clove, minced

1/3 tablespoon fresh ginger, minced

¾ pound skinless, boneless chicken breast, cut into thin strips

2 medium carrots, peeled and spiralized with Blade C

2 medium zucchini, spiralized with Blade C

1 large broccoli stem, spiralized with Blade C

¾ tablespoon honey

¾ tablespoon soy sauce

1/3 tablespoon Sriracha sauce

Salt and freshly ground black pepper, to taste

Directions:

1. In a large skillet, melt butter on medium heat.
2. Add garlic, ginger and sauté for about 30 seconds.
3. Add chicken and cook for about 5-7 minutes.
4. Add carrot, zucchini and broccoli and cook for about 3-4 minutes.
5. Add honey, soy sauce and Sriracha sauce and cook for about 1 minute.
6. Season with salt and pepper and serve hot.

Garlic Turkey Sweet Potato with Spinach

Time: 25 minutes

Servings: 4

Ingredients:

2 large sweet potatoes, spiralized with Blade C

2 tablespoons olive oil, divided

Salt and freshly ground black pepper, to taste

3 garlic cloves, minced

½ teaspoon red pepper flakes, crushed

1 pound turkey tenderloin, trimmed and cubed

4 cups fresh spinach, torn

½ cup mozzarella cheese, divided

2 tablespoons fresh cilantro leaves, chopped

Directions:

1. Preheat the oven to 425 degrees F.
2. Lightly, grease a large baking sheet.
3. In a large bowl, add sweet potato, 1 tablespoon of oil, salt and black pepper and toss to coat well.
4. Transfer the mixture into prepared baking sheet.
5. Roast for about 6 minutes.
6. Transfer the sweet potato into a large plate.
7. Meanwhile in a large skillet, heat remaining oil on medium heat.
8. Add garlic and red pepper flakes and sauté for about 1 minute.
9. Add turkey and sprinkle with salt and black pepper and stir fry for about 4-5 minutes.
10. Add spinach and cook for about 2-3 minutes.
11. Stir in sweet potato and ¼ cup of cheese and remove from heat.
12. Garnish with remaining cheese and cilantro and serve.

Bell Pepper Zucchini Turkey

Time: 40 minutes

Servings: 4

Ingredients:

2 tablespoons olive oil, divided

2 cups boneless turkey breast, cubed

Salt and freshly ground black pepper, to taste

½ cup yellow onion, chopped

½ cup green bell pepper, seeded and chopped

½ cup red bell pepper, seeded and chopped

½ cup yellow bell pepper, seeded and chopped

½ cup orange bell pepper, seeded and chopped

2 garlic cloves, minced

1 jalapeño pepper, seeded and chopped

½ teaspoon dried oregano, crushed

¼ teaspoon red chili powder

3 large zucchinis, spiralized with Blade C

Directions:

1. *In a large skillet, heat 1 tablespoon of oil on medium heat.*
2. *Add turkey and sprinkle with salt and black pepper and cook for about 6-8 minutes or till done completely.*
3. *Transfer the turkey into a plate.*
4. *In the same skillet, heat remaining oil.*
5. *Add onion and bell peppers and sauté for 5-7 minutes.*

6. Add garlic, jalapeño pepper, oregano and red chili powder and sauté for about 1 minute.

7. Stir in zucchini, salt and black pepper and cook for about 3-4 minutes.

8. Stir in turkey and remove from heat.

9. Serve hot.

Arugula Turkey & Sweet Potato with

Time: 35 minutes

Servings: 2

Ingredients:

1 tablespoon olive oil

½ cup yellow onion, chopped

2 garlic clove, minced

1 large sweet potatoes, peeled and spiralized with Blade C

Salt and freshly ground black pepper, to taste

1 cup cooked skinless, boneless turkey breast, cut into bite sized pieces

¼ cup chicken broth

3 cups fresh arugula, chopped

1 tablespoon fresh basil, chopped

Directions:

1. In a large skillet, heat oil on medium heat.
2. Add onion and garlic and sauté for about 3 to 4 minute.
3. Add sweet potato noodles and sprinkle with salt and black pepper and cook for about 2-3 minutes.
4. Add cooked turkey and broth and cook for about 2-3 minutes.
5. Add arugula and basil and cook for about 2-3 minutes.
6. Serve hot.

Mushroom Zucchini Turkey

Time: 50 minutes

Servings: 4

Ingredients:

2 tablespoons olive oil, divided

1 cup white onion, chopped

1 pound lean ground turkey

2 garlic cloves, minced

1 cup shiitake mushrooms, sliced

1 pound lean ground turkey

4 cups Roma tomatoes, chopped

Salt and freshly ground black pepper, to taste

1 cup chicken broth

3 large zucchinis, spiralized with Blade C

½ cup fresh parsley, chopped

Directions:

1. In a large skillet, heat 1 tablespoon of oil on medium heat.
2. Add onion and sauté for about 4-5 minutes.
3. Add garlic and sauté for about 1 minute.
4. Add mushrooms and cook for 4-5 minutes.
5. Add turkey and cook for about 5-6 minutes.
6. Add tomatoes, salt and black pepper and cook for 2-3 minutes, crushing with the back of spoon.
7. Add broth and bring to a boil.
8. Reduce the heat to medium-low and simmer for about 10-15 minutes.
9. Meanwhile in another skillet, heat remaining oil on medium heat.
10. Add zucchini, salt and black pepper and cook for about 4-5 minutes.
11. Transfer the zucchini into large serving plate and top with turkey gravy.
12. Garnish with parsley and serve hot.

Turkey Meatballs With Zucchini Spinach

Time: 35 minutes

Servings: 2

Ingredients:

For Meatballs:

½ pound lean ground turkey

1½ tablespoons coconut milk

1 tablespoon coconut flour

¼ teaspoon dried oregano, crushed

¼ teaspoon dried thyme, crushed

Salt and freshly ground black pepper, to taste

For Zucchini:

2 large zucchinis, spiralized with Blade C

3 cups fresh spinach, chopped

1 garlic clove, minced

3 tablespoons walnuts, chopped

2 tablespoons almond butter

3 tablespoons olive oil

1½ tablespoons fresh lemon juice

3 tablespoons water

Salt and freshly ground black pepper, to taste

Directions:

1. Preheat the oven to 400 degrees F.
2. Line a baking sheet with a parchment paper.
3. For meatballs in a large bowl, add all ingredients and mix till well combined.
4. Make desired size balls from mixture.
5. Arrange the meatballs in prepared baking sheet in a single layer.
6. Bake for about 12-15 minutes or till done completely.
7. Meanwhile in a large serving bowl, place the zucchini noodles.
8. In a food processor, add all remaining ingredients and pulse till smooth.
9. Pour spinach mixture over the zucchini and gently toss to coat.
10. Top with meatballs and serve.

Tomatoes Duck Zucchini

Time: 2 hours 15 minutes

Servings: 4

Ingredients:

For Duck:

1 (5-pound) whole duck

2 teaspoons cayenne pepper

Salt and freshly ground black pepper, to taste

½ cup butter, melted and divided

For Zucchini:

4 large zucchinis, spiralized with Blade C

1½ cups grape tomatoes, halved

1 tablespoons extra virgin olive oil

1 garlic clove, minced

1 cup fresh basil leaves, chopped

Salt and freshly ground black pepper, to taste

Directions:

1. Preheat the oven to 375 degrees F.
2. Line a roasting pan with a parchment paper.
3. Arrange duck in prepared roasting pan and rub with cayenne pepper, salt and black pepper generously.
4. Roast for about 1 hour.
5. Pour half of melted butter over duck and roast for about 45 minutes.
6. Now, pour remaining butter over duck and roast for about 15 minutes more.
7. Remove the duck from oven and transfer onto a cutting board.
8. Keep aside for about 15 minutes.
9. With a sharp knife cut into desired size pieces.
10. Meanwhile in a large serving bowl, place zucchini noodles and remaining ingredients and mix.
11. Top with sliced duck and serve immediately.

Chapter 3 SPIRALIZER SALAD RECIPES

Pecan Apple & Carrot Salad

Time: 15 minutes

Servings: 2

Ingredients:

For Salad:

1 large carrot, peeled and spiralized with Blade C

1 large apple, spiralized with Blade C

1 cup fresh cranberries

2 cups fresh baby arugula

½ cup pecans, chopped

For Dressing:

1 garlic clove, minced

2 tablespoons apple cider Vinegar

tablespoons Extra Virgin Olive Oil

1 tablespoon Honey

1 tablespoon Soy Sauce

Salt and freshly ground black pepper, to taste

Directions:

1. In a large serving bowl, add all salad ingredients except pecans and mix.

2. In another bowl, add all dressing ingredients and beat till well combined.

3. Pour dressing over salad and toss to coat well. Top with pecans and serve.

Parmesan Apple & Scallion Salad

Time: 15 minutes

Servings: 4

Ingredients:

For Salad:

4 medium Pink Lady apples, spiralized with Blade C

½ cup scallion, chopped finely

½ cup Parmesan cheese, shredded

For Dressing:

1 small garlic clove, minced

1 tablespoon extra-virgin olive oil

2 tablespoons fresh lemon juice

1 teaspoon Dijon mustard

Salt and freshly ground black pepper, to taste

Directions:

1. *In a large serving bowl, add all salad ingredients.*
2. *In another bowl, add all dressing ingredients and beat till well combined.*
3. *Pour dressing over salad and toss to coat well.*
4. *Serve immediately.*

Walnut Apple & Basil Salad

Time: 20 minutes

Servings: 2

Ingredients:

For Salad:

2 medium Fuji apples, spiralized with Blade C

1 tablespoon fresh basil, julienned

2 tablespoons walnuts, toasted and chopped

For Dressing:

1 tablespoon shallot, minced

3 tablespoons walnut oil

1 tablespoon apple cider vinegar

Salt and freshly ground black pepper, to taste

Directions:

1. In a large serving bowl, add all salad ingredients.
2. In another bowl, add all dressing ingredients and beat till well combined.
3. Pour dressing over salad and toss to coat well.
4. Serve immediately.

Spinach Apple & Greens Salad

Time: 20 minutes

Servings: 6

Ingredients:

1 large bunch fresh kale, trimmed and chopped

Salt, to taste

1 medium apple, spiralized with Blade C

1 medium cucumber, spiralized with Blade C

4 cups fresh baby spinach

2 tablespoons olive oil

1 tablespoon apple cider vinegar

1 tablespoon mustard

2 tablespoons fresh apple juice

½ cup almonds, chopped

Directions:

1. In a medium bowl, add the kale and salt and with your hands, massage till leaves become tender.
2. In a large serving bowl, mix together kale, apple, cucumber and spinach.
3. In another bowl, add remaining ingredients except almonds and beat till well combined.
4. Pour dressing over salad and toss to coat well.
5. Serve immediately with the topping of almonds.

Yummy Pear & Brussels Sprout Salad

Time: 20 minutes

Servings: 4

Ingredients:

For Salad:

2 Anjou pears, spiralized with Blade C

2 cups Brussels sprout, trimmed and sliced thinly

2 cups fresh kale, trimmed and chopped finely

½ cup almonds, chopped

For Dressing:

1 tablespoon shallot, minced

2 tablespoons apple cider vinegar

2 tablespoons extra-virgin olive oil

1 tablespoon pure maple syrup

1 teaspoons Dijon mustard

Salt and freshly ground black pepper, to taste

Directions:

1. In a large serving bowl, add all salad ingredients except walnuts and mix.

2. In another bowl, add all dressing ingredients and beat till well combined.

3. Pour dressing over salad and toss to coat well.

4. Top with walnuts and serve.

Yogurt Dill Cucumber Salad

Time: 10 minutes

Servings: 2

Ingredients:

½ cup plain Greek yogurt

1 tablespoon fresh lemon juice

2 garlic cloves, minced

1 tablespoon fresh dill, minced

Salt, to taste

2 medium cucumbers, spiralized with Blade C

Directions:

1. In a large serving bowl, add all ingredients except cucumbers and beat till well combined.
2. Add carrots and gently toss to coat well.

Cucumber & Melon Salad

Time: 15 minutes

Servings: 4

Ingredients:

For Salad:

1 large cucumber, spiralized with Blade C

1 cup avocado, peeled, pitted and cubed

2 cups honeydew melon, peeled, seeded and cubed

½ cup feta cheese, crumbled

For Vinaigrette:

1 tablespoon fresh mint leaves, minced

2 teaspoons pure maple syrup

1½ tablespoons balsamic vinegar

1 tablespoon extra-virgin olive oil

2 teaspoons fresh lemon juice

Salt and freshly ground black pepper, to taste

Directions:

1. *In a large serving bowl, add all salad ingredients and mix.*
2. *In another bowl, add all dressing ingredients and beat till well combined.*
3. *Pour dressing over salad and toss to coat well.*
4. *Serve immediately.*

Dijon Mustard Cucumber & Egg Salad

Time: 25 minutes

Servings: 2

Ingredients:

For Dressing:

1 garlic clove, minced

2/3 cup plain yogurt

½ tablespoon Dijon mustard

Salt and freshly ground black pepper, to taste

For Salad:

2 medium cucumbers, spiralized with Blade C

2 large hard boiled eggs, peeled and chopped

½ cup celery, chopped

1 tablespoon almonds, toasted and chopped

Directions:

1. *In a bowl, add all dressing ingredients and beat till well combined.*
2. *In a large serving bowl, mix together cucumber, eggs and celery.*
3. *Pour dressing over salad and toss to coat well.*
4. *Top with almonds and serve.*

Walnut Cucumber & Tomato Salad

Time: 20 minutes

Servings: 2

Ingredients:

2 small cucumbers, peeled and spiralized with Blade C

1 cup cherry tomatoes, halved

½ cup red onion, chopped

¼ cup black olives, pitted and halved

2 cups fresh baby greens

1 tablespoon extra-virgin olive oil

1 tablespoon fresh lime juice

Salt and freshly ground black pepper, to taste

¼ cup walnuts, chopped

Directions:

1. In a large serving bowl, add all ingredients except walnuts and toss to coat well.

2. Top with walnuts and serve.

Spinach Cucumber & Asparagus Salad

Time: 25 minutes

Servings: 2

Ingredients:

1 bunch asparagus, trimmed and cut into 2-inch slices

1 cup fresh spinach, torn

2 cucumbers, peeled and spiralized with Blade C

1 teaspoon fresh ginger, grated

2 scallions, chopped

2 tablespoons extra virgin olive oil

1½ tablespoons tamari

1/8 teaspoon cayenne pepper

Salt and freshly ground black pepper, to taste

2 tablespoons sesame seeds, toasted

Directions:

1. *In a pan of salted boiling water, add asparagus and spinach and cook for about 2-3 minutes.*
2. *Drain and immediately place into a bowl of ice water.*
3. *Drain well.*
4. *In a large serving bowl, place asparagus, spinach and cucumbers.*
5. *In another bowl, add remaining ingredients except sesame seeds and beat till well combined.*
6. *Pour ginger mixture over veggies and toss to coat well.*
7. *Top with sesame seeds and serve immediately.*

Peanut Butter Cucumber & Carrot Salad

Time: 25 minutes

Servings: 2

Ingredients:

For Salad:

½ cup cucumber, peeled and spiralized with Blade C

½ cup carrot, peeled and spiralized with Blade C

1 cup fresh spinach, torn

¼ cup red onion, chopped

For Dressing:

¼ cup creamy peanut butter

¼ cup warm water

1 tablespoon honey

½ tablespoon soy sauce ½ teaspoon fresh ginger, minced

1 garlic clove, minced

Pinch of red pepper flakes, crushed

Directions:

1. In a large bowl, add all salad ingredients and mix.
2. In another bowl, add all dressing ingredients and beat till well combined.
3. Pour dressing over salad and toss to coat well.
4. Serve immediately.

Cucumber, Onion & Pimentos Salad

Time: 20 minutes

Servings: 4

Ingredients:

6 medium cucumbers, peeled and spiralized with Blade C

1 medium sweet onion, peeled and spiralized with Blade C

1 (4-ounce) jar diced pimientos, drained

1 cup sugar

1 cup white vinegar

1 cup water

Salt and freshly ground black pepper, to taste

1 tablespoon fresh dill, minced

Directions:

1. *In a large bowl, mix together cucumbers, onion and pimentos.*
2. *In another bowl, add remaining ingredients and beat till sugar is dissolved.*
3. *Pour dressing over salad and toss to coat well.*
4. *Serve immediately.*

Honey Cucumber & Onion Salad

Time: 20 minutes

Servings: 4

Ingredients:

3 large cucumbers, peeled and spiralized with Blade C

1 red onion, sliced thinly

¼ cup fresh lemon juice

2 tablespoons Filtered Water

2 teaspoons Raw Honey

Salt and freshly ground black pepper, to taste

2 teaspoons sesame seeds

Directions:

1. In a large serving bowl, place cucumbers noodles and onion.

2. In another bowl, add remaining ingredients except sesame seeds and beat till well combined.

3. Pour honey mixture over veggies and toss to coat well.

4. Cover and refrigerate to chill completely.

5. Top with sesame seeds and serve.

Cucumber & Avocado Beet Salad

Time: 20 minutes

Servings: 2

Ingredients:

2 medium beets, peeled and spiralized with Blade C

1 large cucumber, peeled and spiralized with Blade C

1 ripe avocado, peeled, pitted and chopped

2 garlic cloves, minced

¼ cup hemp seeds

1 tablespoon tamari

1 tablespoon walnut oil

2 tablespoons fresh lemon juice

1/8 teaspoon cayenne pepper

Salt and freshly ground black pepper, to taste

Directions:

1. *In a large serving bowl, place the beets and cucumbers.*
2. *In a food processor, add remaining ingredients and pulse till smooth.*
3. *Pour avocado mixture over vegetables and toss to coat well.*
4. *Serve immediately.*

Ginger Carrot Salad in Basil Sauce

Time: 15 minutes

Servings: 2

Ingredients:

2 large carrots, peeled and spiralized with Blade C

1 medium green bell pepper, seeded and chopped

1 teaspoon fresh ginger, grated

1 garlic clove, minced

½ cup fresh cilantro leaves, chopped

2 tablespoons extra virgin olive oil

1 tablespoon fresh lemon juice

1 teaspoon tamari

2 tablespoons sesame seeds

Directions:

1. In a large bowl, add the carrots and bell pepper.

2. In a food processor, add remaining ingredients except sesame seeds and pulse till smooth.

3. Pour the dressing over carrots and toss to coat well.

4. Top with sesame seeds and serve.

Chickpeas Zucchini & Carrot Salad

Time: 15 minutes

Servings: 2

Ingredients:

For Salad:

1 medium zucchini, spiralized with Blade C

1 small carrot, peeled and spiralized with Blade C

¼ cup cherry tomatoes, halved

½ cup cooked chickpeas

For Dressing:

¼ cup mayonnaise

2 tablespoons maple syrup

1 tablespoon fresh lime juice

1 teaspoon extra virgin olive oil

2 teaspoons fresh parsley, minced

Salt and freshly ground black pepper, to taste

Directions:

1. In a large serving bowl, add all salad ingredients and mix.
2. In another bowl, add all dressing ingredients and beat till well combined.
3. Pour dressing over salad and toss to coat well.
4. Serve immediately.

Raisins Zucchini & Berries Salad

Time: 25 minutes

Servings: 4

Ingredients:

1 large zucchini, spiralized with Blade C

1 large carrot, peeled and spiralized with Blade C

½ cup fresh strawberries, hulled and sliced

¼ cup fresh raspberries

¼ cup fresh blueberries

¼ cup fresh blackberries

2 cups fresh baby spinach

½ cup golden raisins

½ cup almonds, toasted and chopped

1 tablespoon extra-virgin olive oil

2 tablespoons fresh lime juice

Salt and freshly ground black pepper, to taste

¼ cup fresh mint leaves, chopped

Directions:

1. In a large serving bowl, add all ingredients except mint and toss to coat well.

2. Garnish with mint and serve immediately.

Pomegranate Zucchini Pear Salad

Time: 15 minutes

Servings: 2

Ingredients:

For Salad:

2 medium zucchinis, spiralized with Blade C

1 large pear, cored and chopped

3 tablespoons fresh pomegranate arils

2 tablespoons fresh mint leaves, chopped

2 tablespoons walnuts, chopped

For Dressing:

¼ cup fresh pomegranate juice

1 teaspoon honey

2 tablespoons fresh lemon juice

1 tablespoon extra-virgin olive oil

Salt and freshly ground black pepper, to taste

Directions:

1. In a large serving bowl, mix together zucchini, pear and pomegranate seeds.

2. In another bowl, add all dressing ingredients and mix till well combined.

3. Pour dressing over salad and toss to coat well.

4. Garnish with mint and walnuts and serve immediately.

Honey Zucchini & Cranberry Salad

Time: 15 minutes

Servings: 2

Ingredients:

For Salad:

2 medium zucchinis, spiralized with Blade C

4 cups romaine lettuce, torn

½ cup fresh cranberries

1 tablespoon fresh mint leaves, chopped

¼ cup walnuts, toasted and chopped

For Dressing:

1 tablespoon extra-virgin olive oil

1 tablespoon fresh lime juice

½ tablespoon honey

Salt and freshly ground black pepper, to taste

Directions:

1. In a large serving bowl, mix together all salad ingredients except walnuts.

2. In another bowl, add all dressing ingredients and beat till well combined.

3. Pour dressing over salad and gently toss to coat well.

4. Garnish with walnuts and serve immediately.

Almond Zucchini Salad in Mango Sauce

Time: 15 minutes

Servings: 4

Ingredients:

1 cup fresh mango, peeled, pitted and cubed

½ cup almond butter

1 teaspoon honey

2 teaspoons fresh lemon juice

2 large zucchinis, spiralized with Blade C

¼ cup almonds, chopped

Directions:

1. In a blender, add mango, butter, honey and lemon juice and pulse till smooth.

2. In a large serving bowl, place zucchini.

3. Add mango sauce and mix well.

4. Top with almonds and serve immediately.

Spicy Almond Butter Sauce Zucchini Salad

Time: 15 minutes

Servings: 2

Ingredients:

1 medium zucchini, spiralized with Blade C

1 medium yellow squash, spiralized with Blade C

1 small red bell pepper, seeded and sliced thinly

1 garlic clove, minced

½ teaspoon fresh ginger, minced

2 tablespoons almond butter

½ tablespoon soy sauce

1 tablespoon fresh lime juice

½ tablespoon Filtered Water

¼ teaspoon red chili powder

Salt and freshly ground black pepper, to taste

1 tablespoon sesame seeds, toasted

Directions:

1. In a lag serving bowl, mix together zucchini, yellow squash and bell pepper.

2. In another small bowl, add remaining ingredients except sesame seeds and beat till well combined.

3. Pour sauce over vegetables and mix well.

4. Top with sesame seeds and serve immediately.

Kale Broccoli Zucchini Salad

Time: 20 minutes

Servings: 4

Ingredients:

3-4 zucchinis, spiralized with Blade C

2 garlic cloves, minced

½ cup broccoli florets, chopped

2 cups fresh kale, trimmed and torn

½ cup fresh cilantro leaves, chopped

2 tablespoons fresh lemon juice

Salt and freshly ground black pepper, to taste

Directions:

1. In a large serving bowl, place the zucchini.

2. In a food processor, add remaining ingredients and pulse till smooth.

3. Pour kale mixture over zucchini and toss to coat well.

4. Serve immediately.

Delicious Zucchini & Cucumber Salad in Sweet & Spicy Sauce

Time: 20 minutes

Servings: 2

Ingredients:

1 zucchini, peeled and spiralized with Blade C

1 cucumber, peeled and spiralized with Blade C

¼ cup almond butter

1 tablespoon fresh lemon juice

1 tablespoon honey

1 tablespoon tamari

2 tablespoons water

1/8 teaspoon cayenne pepper, crushed

Salt and freshly ground black pepper, to taste

2 tablespoons Almonds, chopped

Directions:

1. In a large colander, place the zucchini and cucumber.
2. Arrange colander over a large bowl and keep aside for at least 15-20 minutes.
3. Gently, squeeze the veggies and pat dry with a paper towel.
4. Transfer the veggies into a large serving bowl.
5. In another bowl, add remaining ingredients except almonds and beat till well combined.
6. Pour honey mixture over veggies and toss to coat well. Top with almonds and serve immediately.

Parsley Cabbage Salad

Time: 15 minutes

Servings: 4

Ingredients:

2½ cups green cabbage, spiralized with Blade C

2½ cups purple cabbage, spiralized with Blade C

2 large scallions, chopped

¼ cup fresh parsley, chopped

1 jalapeño pepper, seeded and chopped finely

2 tablespoons fresh lemon juice

2 tablespoons extra-virgin olive oil

Salt, to taste

1 teaspoon fresh lemon zest, grated finely

Directions:

1. In a large serving bowl, add all ingredients except lemon zest and toss to coat well.

2. Top with lemon zest and serve.

Kale Cabbage & Carrot Salad

Time: 15 minutes

Servings: 2

Ingredients:

For Salad:

1 large carrot, peeled and spiralized with Blade C

1 cup purple cabbage, spiralized with Blade C

2 cups fresh baby kale, trimmed

2 tablespoons red onion, chopped

2 tablespoons fresh mint leaves, chopped

For Dressing:

1 tablespoon extra-virgin olive oil

1 teaspoon apple cider vinegar

2 tablespoons sunflower seeds

Salt and freshly ground black pepper, to taste

Directions:

1. In a large serving bowl, add all salad ingredients and mix.

2. In another bowl, add all dressing ingredients and beat till well combined.

3. Pour dressing over salad and toss to coat well.

4. Serve immediately.

Crumbled Fetta Cheese Honey Beet Salad

Time: 10 minutes

Servings: 2

Ingredients:

For Salad:

2 medium beets, trimmed, peeled and spiralized with Blade C

2 tablespoons feta cheese, crumbled

For Dressing:

2 tablespoons fresh orange juice

1 tablespoon extra-virgin olive oil

1 tablespoon balsamic vinegar

½ tablespoon honey

Salt and freshly ground black pepper, to taste

Directions:

1. In a large bowl, place the beets.
2. In another bowl, add all dressing ingredients and beat till well combined.
3. Pour dressing over salad and toss to coat well.
4. Serve immediately with the topping of feta cheese.

Sesame Beet & Avocado Salad

Time: 15 minutes

Servings: 2

Ingredients:

For Salad:

2 medium beets, trimmed, peeled and spiralized with Blade C

1 small avocado, peeled, pitted and chopped

1 tablespoon sesame seeds

For Dressing:

1 teaspoon fresh ginger, minced

1 garlic clove, minced

2 tablespoons fresh cilantro, minced

¼ cup fresh lemon juice

3 tablespoons extra-virgin olive oil

2 teaspoons soy sauce

2 drops liquid stevia

Directions:

1. In a large serving bowl, add beets and avocado.
2. In another bowl, add all dressing ingredients and beat till well combined.
3. Pour dressing over salad and toss to coat well.
4. Serve immediately with a topping of sesame seeds.

Fresh Mint Beet & Cashew Salad

Time: 15 minutes

Servings: 2

Ingredients:

For Salad:

2 large beets, trimmed, peeled and spiralized with Blade C

¼ cup fresh mint leaves, chopped

¼ cup feta cheese, crumbled

¼ cup cashews, chopped

For Dressing:

2 tablespoons balsamic vinegar

2 tablespoons extra-virgin olive oil

1 teaspoon honey

2 teaspoons Dijon mustard

Salt, to taste

Pinch of red pepper flakes, crushed

Directions:

1. *In a large serving bowl, add all salad ingredients and mix.*
2. *In another bowl, add all dressing ingredients and beat till well combined.*
3. *Pour dressing over salad and toss to coat well.*
4. *Serve immediately.*

Pecans Beet & Cherry Salad

Time: 20 minutes

Servings: 2

Ingredients:

For Salad:

2 medium golden beets, trimmed, peeled and spiralized with Blade C

½ pound fresh cherries, pitted and halved

2 cups fresh baby kale

¼ cup pecans, chopped

¼ goat cheese, crumbled

For Dressing:

2 teaspoons shallots, minced

¼ cup extra-virgin olive oil

2 tablespoons fresh lemon juice

2 teaspoons honey

2 teaspoons Dijon mustard

Salt and freshly ground black pepper, to taste

Directions:

1. In a large serving bowl, add all salad ingredients and mix.

2. In another bowl, add all dressing ingredients and beat till well combined.

3. Pour dressing over salad and toss to coat well.

4. Serve immediately.

Yummy Beet & Orange Salad

Time: 15 minutes

Servings: 2

Ingredients:

2 medium golden beets, trimmed, peeled and spiralized with Blade C

2 tablespoons red wine vinegar

1½ tablespoons olive oil

8-ounce canned mandarin oranges, drained, reserving 2 tablespoons of juice

1 tablespoon fresh mint leaves, chopped

Directions:

1. *In a large bowl, place the beets.*
2. *In another bowl, add vinegar, oil and reserved orange juice and mix well.*
3. *Pour juice mixture over beet and toss to coat well and keep aside for about 15 minutes.*
4. *Top with orange and mint and serve.*

Chili Zucchini & Corn Salad

Time: 35 minutes

Servings: 6

Ingredients:

For Salad:

3 ears of corn

1 teaspoon olive oil

Salt and freshly ground black pepper, to taste

2 large zucchinis, spiralized with Blade C

1 medium red onion, chopped

For Dressing:

1 teaspoon fresh lemon zest, grated finely

2 tablespoons extra-virgin olive oil

1 tablespoon balsamic vinegar

1 teaspoon honey

1 teaspoon garlic powder

½ teaspoon chili powder

Salt and freshly ground black pepper, to taste

Directions:

1. Preheat the grill to medium heat.

2. Grease the grill grate.

3. Drizzle the corn ears with olive oil and sprinkle with salt and black pepper.

4. Grill for about 15-20 minutes, flipping after every 5 minutes.
5. Remove from grill and keep aside to cool slightly.
6. Cut the kernels off.
7. In a large bowl, mix together zucchini, corn and onion.
8. In another bowl, add all dressing ingredients and beat till well combined.
9. Pour dressing over salad and toss to coat well.
10. Serve immediately.

Kidney Beans Zucchini Salad

Time: 15 minutes

Servings: 2

Ingredients:

For Salad:

2 medium zucchinis, spiralized with Blade C

1 medium avocado, peeled, pitted and cubed

½ cup red kidney beans

1 tablespoon scallion, chopped

1 tablespoon fresh cilantro leaves, chopped

1 tablespoon extra-virgin olive oil

1 tablespoon fresh lemon juice

Salt and freshly ground black pepper, to taste

Directions:

1. In a large serving bowl, add all ingredients and gently toss to coat well.
2. Serve immediately.

Cumin Carrot, Zucchini & Chickpeas Salad

Time: 25 minutes

Servings: 3

Ingredients:

1 large orange carrot, peeled and spiralized with Blade C

1 large red carrot, peeled and spiralized with Blade C

2 medium zucchinis, peeled and spiralized with Blade C

¼ cup fresh basil leaves, chopped

1 cup cooked chickpeas

1 tablespoon olive oil

¼ teaspoon chili powder

¼ teaspoon ground cumin

Salt and freshly ground black pepper, to taste

Directions:

1. In a large bowl, add all ingredients and toss to coat well.
2. Serve immediately.

Pine Nuts Zucchini & Quinoa Salad

Time: 25 minutes

Servings: 3

Ingredients:

2 zucchinis, peeled and spiralized with Blade C

½ cup prepared pesto

2 sundried tomatoes, chopped

1/3 cup cooked quinoa

2 tablespoons pine nuts

Directions:

1. In a bowl, add all ingredients except pine nuts and mix till well combined.
2. Top with pine nuts and serve.

Delicious Zucchini & Chicken Salad

Time: 40 minutes

Servings: 4

Ingredients:

For Salad:

2 garlic cloves, minced

2 tablespoons extra virgin coconut oil, melted

½ tablespoon soy sauce

1 tablespoon fresh lime Juice

Salt and freshly ground black pepper, to taste

2 (6-ounce) skinless, boneless chicken breasts, cubed

2 medium zucchinis, spiralized with Blade C

5-6 cups fresh baby greens

½ cup pecans, toasted and chopped

For Dressing:

2 tablespoons shallot, minced

1 tablespoon capers, chopped finely

1 garlic clove, minced

1 jalapeño pepper, seeded and minced

2 tablespoons fresh cilantro leaves, minced

1 teaspoon lime zest, grated freshly

¼ cup extra virgin olive oil

2 teaspoons coconut vinegar

2 tablespoons fresh lime juice

Salt and freshly ground black pepper, to taste

Directions:

1. Preheat the oven to 350 degrees F.
2. Line a baking sheet with a piece of foil.
3. In a large bowl, mix together garlic, oil, soy sauce, lime juice, salt and black pepper.
4. Add chicken cubes and coat with mixture generously.
5. Keep aside for about 15-20 minutes.
6. Transfer the mixture into prepared baking sheet.
7. Bake for about 15- 20 minutes.
8. Transfer the chicken cubes into a large serving bowl and keep aside to cool slightly.
9. Add zucchini and greens.
10. In another bowl, add all dressing ingredients and beat till well combined.
11. Pour dressing over salad and toss to coat well.
12. Top with pecans and serve immediately.

Cashews Zucchini, Carrot & Chicken Salad

Time: 30 minutes

Servings: 2

Ingredients:

For Salad:

1 tablespoon extra-virgin coconut oil

1 (6-ounce) skinless, boneless chicken breast

Salt and freshly ground black pepper, to taste

1 large zucchini, spiralized with Blade C

1 large carrot, spiralized with Blade C

2 tablespoons fresh mint leaves, chopped

2 tablespoons cashews, chopped

For Dressing:

1 garlic clove, minced

½ teaspoon fresh ginger, minced

1 jalapeño pepper, seeded and minced

2 tablespoons coconut cream

1 tablespoon almond butter

½ tablespoon honey

1 tablespoon soy sauce

1 tablespoon fresh lemon juice

Salt and freshly ground black pepper, to taste

Directions:

1. In a skillet, heat oil on medium heat.
2. Add chicken and sprinkle with salt and black pepper.
3. Cook for about 4-5 minutes from both sides or till chicken is done completely.
4. Transfer the chicken into a large plate and keep aside to cool completely.
5. Then shred the chicken and transfer into a large serving bowl.
6. Add zucchini, carrot and mint.
7. In another bowl, add all dressing ingredients and mix till well combined.
8. Pour dressing over salad and gently, mix to coat.
9. Top with pistachios and serve.

Garlic Zucchini, Cucumber & Chicken Salad

Time: 40 minutes

Servings: 4

For Chicken:

2 garlic cloves, minced

1 tablespoon fresh thyme, chopped

2 tablespoons olive oil

2 tablespoons soy sauce

Salt and freshly ground black pepper, to taste

2 skinless, boneless chicken thighs

For Salad:

½ cup cucumber, spiralized with Blade C

½ cup zucchini, spiralized with Blade C

2 cups fresh baby greens

2 tablespoons extra virgin olive oil

2 tablespoons fresh lemon juice

Salt and freshly ground black pepper, to taste

2 tablespoons scallion, chopped

Directions:

1. Preheat the oven broiler.
2. Grease a baking dish.
3. In a large bowl, add all chicken ingredients and toss to coat well.
4. Transfer the chicken mixture into prepared baking dish.
5. Broil for about 20 minutes.
6. Meanwhile in a large serving bowl, add all salad I ingredients except scallion and toss to coat well.
7. Transfer the salad into 2 serving plates.
8. Top with chicken thighs.
9. Garnish with scallion and serve.

Zucchini & Turkey Salad

Time: 25 minutes

Servings: 4

Ingredients:

For Turkey:

2 teaspoons olive oil

2 garlic cloves, minced

1 pound turkey tenderloin, trimmed and cut into thin strips

Salt and freshly ground black pepper, to taste

For Salad:

2 medium zucchinis, spiralized with Blade C

¾ cup black olives, pitted and halved

½ cup red bell pepper, seeded and sliced thinly

For Dressing:

2 garlic cloves, minced

1 teaspoon dried Basil, crushed

3 tablespoons extra virgin olive oil

2 tablespoons balsamic vinegar

2 tablespoons fresh lemon juice

Salt and freshly ground black pepper, to taste

Directions:

1. For Turkey in a large skillet, heat oil on medium-high heat.
2. Add garlic and sauté for about 1 minute.
3. Add turkey and sprinkle with salt and black pepper. Stir fry for about 5-7 minutes.
4. Transfer turkey into a plate.
5. For salad in a large serving bowl, mix together all ingredients.
6. Add turkey and mix well.
7. In another small bowl, add all dressing ingredients and beat till well combined.
8. Pour dressing over salad and toss to coat well.
9. Serve immediately.

Soy Sauce Steak Salad With Carrot, Cucumber

Time: 35 minutes

Servings: 4

Ingredients:

For Steak:

1/3 cup soy sauce

1 tablespoon fresh lemon juice

Salt and freshly ground black pepper, to taste

¾ pound sirloin steak, trimmed

For Salad:

3 zucchinis, spiralized with Blade C

1 medium carrot, peeled and spiralized with Blade C

1 cucumber, spiralized with Blade C

1 red bell pepper, seeded and sliced thinly

2 garlic cloves

¼ cup fresh cilantro leaves, minced

2 tablespoons fresh lemon juice

3 tablespoons extra virgin olive oil

Salt and freshly ground black pepper, to taste

1 teaspoon sesame seeds, toasted

Directions:

1. For steak in a large bowl, mix together all ingredients except steak.
2. Add steak and coat with marinade generously.
3. Refrigerate, covered for at least 6-8 hours.
4. Preheat the grill to medium-high heat.
5. Grease the grill grate.
6. Grill the steak for about 5-6 minutes per side.
7. Remove from grill and transfer onto a cutting board.
8. Keep aside for about 10 minutes.
9. With a sharp knife slice the steak according to your choice.
10. Meanwhile in a large serving bowl, mix together zucchini, carrot, cucumber and bell pepper.
11. In another bowl, add remaining ingredients except sesame seeds and beat till well combined.
12. Pour dressing over vegetables and gently, toss to coat.
13. Top with steak slices.
14. Garnish with sesame seeds and serve.

Radishes Zucchini & Steak Salad

Time: 25 minutes

Servings: 4

Ingredients:

For Salad:

1 (1¼ pounds) flank steak, trimmed

1 tablespoon extra-virgin olive oil

Salt and freshly ground black pepper, to taste

2 large zucchinis, spiralized with Blade C

1 red bell pepper, seeded and sliced thinly

1 orange bell pepper, seeded and sliced thinly

4 radishes, julienned

2 cups romaine lettuce, torn

1 avocado, peeled, pitted and chopped

For Dressing:

1 cup fresh cilantro, chopped

1 cup fresh parsley, chopped

2 garlic cloves, minced

2 jalapeños, seeded and chopped

¼ cup extra-virgin olive oil

¼ cup fresh lemon juice

Salt and freshly ground black pepper, to taste

Directions:

1. Preheat the grill to high.
2. Grease the grill grate.
3. Drizzle the steak with oil and sprinkle with salt and black pepper.
4. Keep aside for about 10-15 minutes.
5. Grill the steak for about 4-5 minutes per side or till desired doneness.
6. Transfer into a plate and keep aside for about 5 minutes before slicing.
7. With a sharp knife, cut the steak into thin slices, diagonally across the grain.
8. Transfer the steak into a large serving bowl.
9. Add remaining salad ingredients except avocado and mix.
10. In a food processor, add all dressing ingredients and pulse till smooth.
11. Pour dressing over salad and toss to coat well.
12. Top with avocado and serve immediately.

Walnut Zucchini & Salmon Salad

Time: 30 minutes

Servings: 4

Ingredients:

For Salmon:

4 (4-ounce) salmon fillets

1 tablespoon extra-virgin olive oil

Salt and freshly ground black pepper, to taste

For Salad:

2 small zucchinis, spiralized with Blade C

1 cup cherry tomatoes, halved

¼ cup black olives, pitted and sliced

3 tablespoons extra-virgin olive oil

3 tablespoon fresh lime juice

2 teaspoons fresh lime zest, grated finely

¼ cup fresh cilantro leaves, minced

Salt and freshly ground black pepper, to taste

¼ cup walnuts, toasted and chopped

Directions:

1. Preheat the grill to high.
2. Grease the grill grate.
3. Drizzle the salmon fillets with oil and sprinkle with salt and black pepper.
4. Grill the salmon fillets for about 4 minutes per side.
5. Remove from grill and transfer into a bowl.
6. In a large serving bowl, mix together zucchini, tomatoes and olives.
7. In another small bowl, add oil, lime juice, zest, cilantro, salt and black pepper and beat till well combined.
8. Pour dressing over salad and toss to coat well.
9. Top with salmon and walnuts and serve immediately.

Zucchini, Cucumber & Salmon Salad

Time: 20 minutes

Servings: 2

Ingredients:

½ cup grilled salmon, cut into bite size pieces

1 medium zucchini, spiralized with Blade C

1 medium cucumber, peeled and spiralized with Blade C

½ cup celery stalk, chopped

½ cup coconut milk

1 small garlic clove, minced

Salt and freshly ground black pepper, to taste

2 hard boiled large eggs, peeled and chopped

Directions:

1. In a large serving bowl, mix together salmon, zucchini, cucumber and celery.

2. In another bowl, add coconut milk, garlic and seasoning and mix till well combined.

3. Pour coconut milk mixture over vegetables and gently, toss to coat.

4. Top with chopped eggs and serve.

Yummy Cod Salad

Time: 35 minutes

Servings: 4

Ingredients:

For Cod:

1 teaspoon ground coriander

1 teaspoon ground cumin

Salt and freshly ground black pepper, to taste

¼ cup fresh lemon juice

4 (4-ounce) cod fillets

For Salad:

1 large carrot, peeled and spiralized with Blade C

1 large cucumber, peeled and spiralized with Blade C

1 (15-ounce) can chickpeas, rinsed and drained

1 cup cherry tomatoes, quartered

1 small red onion, chopped

For Dressing:

1 garlic clove, minced

1 teaspoon fresh lemon zest, grated finely

2 tablespoons extra-virgin olive oil

2 tablespoons fresh lemon juice

¾ teaspoon curry powder

Salt and freshly ground black pepper, to taste

Directions:

1. Preheat the oven to 400 degrees F.
2. Lightly, grease shallow baking dish.
3. For cod in a bowl, add all ingredients and toss to coat well.
4. Arrange the cod fillets onto prepared baking dish.
5. Bake for about 15 minutes.
6. In a large bowl, mix together all salad ingredients.
7. In another small bowl, add all dressing ingredients and beat till well combined.
8. Pour dressing over salad and toss to coat well.
9. Top with cod fillets and serve immediately.

Zucchini & Sardine Salad

Time: 25 minutes

Servings: 4

Ingredients:

For Sardines:

3 garlic cloves, minced

1 teaspoon dried rosemary, crushed

¼ cup fresh lemon juice

¼ cup extra-virgin olive oil

¼ teaspoon cayenne pepper

Salt and freshly ground black pepper, to taste

1 pound fresh sardines, scaled and gutted

For Vegetables:

3-4 zucchinis, spiralized with Blade C

½ cup fresh baby arugula

¼ cup cherry tomatoes, halved

2 tablespoons black olives, pitted and halved

1 garlic clove, minced

½ teaspoon fresh lemon zest, grated finely

2 tablespoons fresh lemon juice

2 tablespoons extra-virgin olive oil

Salt and freshly ground black pepper, to taste

Directions:

3. For sardines in a bowl, mix together all ingredients except sardines.
4. Place sardines in a large shallow dish in a single layer.
5. Coat the sardines with garlic mixture evenly.
6. Cover and keep aside to marinate for at least 1 hour.
7. Preheat the grill to high heat.
8. Grease the grill grate.
9. Grill the sardines for about 5 minutes on direct heat, flipping once after 3 minutes.
10. Remove from grill and keep aside to cool.
11. Then, cut into bite size pieces.

12. Meanwhile in a large serving bowl, mix together zucchini, arugula, olives and tomatoes.
13. In another bowl, add remaining ingredients and beat till well combined.
14. Pour lemon mixture over veggies and toss to coat well.
15. Top with sardine pieces and serve.

Ginger Zucchini & Shrimp Salad

Time: 25 minutes

Servings: 2

Ingredients:

For Salad:

1 tablespoon extra-virgin Olive Oil

2 garlic cloves, minced

1 teaspoon fresh ginger, minced

½ pound shrimp, peeled and deveined

Salt and freshly ground black pepper, to taste

2 medium zucchinis, spiralized with Blade C

3 cups mixed fresh baby greens

1 small avocado, peeled, pitted and chopped

For Dressing:

1 tablespoon extra-virgin olive oil

1 tablespoon fresh lemon juice

1 tablespoon soy sauce

½ teaspoon honey

Pinch of red pepper flakes, crushed

Salt and freshly ground black pepper, to taste

Directions:

1. In a skillet, heat oil on medium heat.
2. Add garlic and ginger and sauté for about 1 minute.
3. Add shrimp and sprinkle with salt and black pepper.
4. Cook for about 4 minutes, flipping once after 2 minutes.
5. Transfer the shrimp into a large serving bowl.
6. Add zucchini and greens with shrimp.
7. In another bowl, add all dressing ingredients and beat till well combined.
8. Pour dressing over salad and gently toss to coat.
9. Garnish with avocado and serve immediately.

CHAPTER 4 STEW & SOUP SPIRALIZER RECIPES

Yummy Zucchini & Roasted Tomato Soup

Time: 45 minutes

Servings: 2

Ingredients:

10 campari tomatoes, halved

2 tablespoons olive oil, divided

Salt and freshly ground black pepper, to taste

1 onion, chopped

2 garlic cloves, minced

¼ teaspoon red pepper flakes, crushed

1 cup vegetable broth

2 tablespoons fresh basil, chopped

1 zucchini, spiralized with Blade C

2 tablespoons plain Greek yogurt

Directions:

1. Preheat the oven to 375 degrees F.

2. Drizzle the tomatoes with 1 tablespoon of oil and sprinkle with salt and black pepper.

3. Arrange the tomato halves onto a baking dish, cut side up.

4. Roast for about 20 minutes.

5. Meanwhile in a large pan, heat the remaining oil on medium heat.

6. Add onion and sauté for about 2-3 minutes.

7. Add garlic and red pepper flakes and sauté for about 1 minute.

8. In a food processor, add onion mixture and roasted tomatoes and pulse till smooth.

9. Return the pureed soup in pan on medium heat.

10. Add broth and basil and bring to a boil.

11. Reduce the heat and simmer for about 10 minutes.

12. Add zucchini and simmer for about 2 minutes.

13. Stir in yogurt and simmer for about 1 minute.

14. Season with salt and black pepper and serve hot.

Onion Zucchini & Bok Choy Soup

Time: 35 minutes

Servings: 2

Ingredients:

7-ounce baby bok choy, trimmed and leaves separated

½ tablespoon yellow miso paste

2 teaspoons sesame oil, divided

½ of yellow onion, sliced thinly

2 scallions, chopped (white and green parts separated)

1 garlic clove, minced

1 (1-inch) piece fresh ginger, minced

2 tablespoons soy sauce

4 cups vegetable broth

3½-ounce shiitake mushrooms, halved

1 large zucchini, spiralized with Blade C

½ teaspoon sesame seeds

Directions:

1. Rub the bok choy leaves with miso paste till covered completely.
2. In a large pan, heat 1 teaspoon of oil on medium-high heat.
3. Add the bok choy and cook for about 3 minutes per side or till charred.
4. Transfer the bok choy into a bowl and keep aside.
5. In the same pan, heat the remaining sesame oil on medium heat.
6. Add onion, white part of scallions, garlic and ginger and sauté for about 5 minutes.
7. Add soy sauce and the broth and bring to the boil.
8. Stir in the mushrooms and reduce the heat to low.
9. Simmer for about 5 minutes.
10. Add the zucchini and cook for about 2-3 minutes.
11. With pasta tongs, carefully transfer the noodles into serving bowls and top with the cooked bok choy.
12. Pour hot soup over the veggies evenly.
13. Serve hot with the garnishing green part of scallions and sesame seeds.

Scallion Zucchini & Asparagus Soup

Time: 25 minutes

Servings: 2

Ingredients:

2 cups vegetable broth

2 miso soup packets

12-16 asparagus spears, trimmed and halved

1 large zucchini, spiralized with Blade C

1 teaspoon Sriracha

2 scallions, chopped

1 tablespoon sesame seeds

Directions:

1. In a medium pan, add 2 cups of broth and bring to a boil.
2. Add miso soup packets and stir to combine.
3. Stir in asparagus spears and bring to a boil.
4. Boil for about 1 minute.
5. Reduce the heat to low and stir in zucchini noodles.
6. Simmer for about 4 minutes.
7. Stir in Sriracha and remove from heat.
8. Serve hot with the garnishing of sesame seeds and scallions.

Healthy Radish & Mushroom Soup

Time: 35 minutes

Servings: 2

Ingredients:

2 teaspoons olive oil

1 red onion, sliced thinly

1 garlic clove, minced

1 (1-inch) piece fresh ginger, minced

2 tablespoons soy sauce

4 cups vegetable broth

1 large Portobello mushroom cap, sliced

1 medium daikon radish, trimmed and spiralized with Blade C

3 cups fresh kale, trimmed and chopped

1 scallion, chopped

½ teaspoon sesame seeds

Directions:

1. In a large pan, heat oil on medium-high heat.
2. Add onion, garlic and ginger and sauté for about 5 minutes.
3. Add soy sauce and the broth and bring to the boil.
4. Stir in the mushroom caps and reduce the heat to low.
5. Simmer for about 5 minutes.
6. Add the radish and kale and cook for about 5-7 minutes.
7. Serve hot with the garnishing of scallions and sesame seeds.

Soy Sauce Zucchini & Tofu Soup

Time: 25 minutes

Servings: 4

Ingredients:

4 green tea bags

3 cups boiling water

2 teaspoons sesame oil

1 teaspoon fresh ginger, minced

1 cup tofu, cubed

3 cups vegetable broth

1 tablespoon miso paste

3 medium zucchinis, spiralized with Blade C

¾ cup scallions, chopped

2 teaspoons soy sauce

Freshly ground black pepper, to taste

Directions:

1. In a bowl, steep the tea bags in boiling water for about 3-4 minutes.

2. Remove the tea bags and keep the broth aside.

3. In a large soup pan, heat oil on medium heat and sauté ginger for about 30 seconds.

4. Add tofu, broth and green tea broth and bring to a boil.

5. Transfer 1bout 1/3 cup of the hot soup into a bowl.

6. Add miso paste and stir to combine.

7. Add miso paste mixture into soup and bring to a boil.

8. Reduce the heat to low.
9. Add remaining ingredients and simmer for about 2-3 minutes.
10. Serve hot.

Thyme Turnip & Lentil Soup

Time: 55 minutes

Servings: 6

Ingredients:

2 tablespoons extra-virgin olive oil

1 medium onion, chopped

2 carrots, peeled and chopped

2 celery ribs, chopped

Salt and freshly ground black pepper, to taste

3 garlic cloves, minced

½ teaspoon dried basil

½ teaspoon dried thyme

½ teaspoon dried oregano

½ teaspoon red pepper flakes, crushed

1 (28-ounce) can diced tomatoes

2 bay leaves

1 cup red lentils, rinsed

6 cups vegetable broth

2 small turnips, peeled and spiralized with Blade C

2 teaspoons fresh lemon juice

Directions:

1. In a large pan, heat oil on medium heat.

2. Add onion, carrot, celery, salt and black pepper and sauté for about 4-5 minutes.

3. Add garlic, herbs and red pepper flakes and sauté for about 1 minute.

4. Add tomatoes and stir till well combined.

5. Add bay leaves, lentils, broth, salt and black pepper and stir well.

6. Increase the heat to high and bring to a boil.

7. Reduce the heat to medium-low and simmer, covered partially for about 20 minutes.

8. Discard the bay leaves and stir in the turnip noodles.

9. Cook for about 5-7 minutes.

10. Stir in lemon juice and serve hot.

Chili Butternut Squash & Cannelini Beans Soup

Time: 45 minutes

Servings: 6

Ingredients:

½ tablespoon extra-virgin olive oil

1 yellow onion, chopped

2 celery stalks, chopped

1 garlic clove

17-ounce canned whole, peeled tomatoes

6 cups vegetable broth

½ teaspoon dried oregano, crushed

¼ teaspoon red chili powder

1 butternut squash, peeled and spiralized with Blade C

1 large bunch fresh kale, trimmed and chopped

1 cup canned white cannelloni beans, rinsed and drained

2 teaspoons fresh chives, chopped

Salt and freshly ground black pepper, to taste

3 tablespoons Parmesan cheese, grated

Directions:

1. In a large pan, heat oil on medium heat.

2. Add onions and celery and sauté for about 4-5 minutes.

3. Add garlic and sauté for about 1 minute.

4. Add tomatoes and cook, chopping the tomatoes with the back of a wooden spoon.

5. Add broth, oregano and red chili powder and bring to a boil.

6. Stir in squash, kale, white beans and chives and reduce the heat to low.

7. Simmer, covered for about 20 minutes.

8. Stir in salt and black pepper and remove from heat.

9. Serve hot with the topping of Parmesan cheese.

Carrot & Cannellini Beans Soup

Time: 50 minutes

Servings: 4

Ingredients:

1 tablespoon extra-virgin olive oil

1 large celery stalk, chopped

1 small yellow onion, chopped

2 garlic cloves, minced

1 (15-ounce) can crushed tomatoes

1 tablespoon fresh thyme leaves, chopped

1 tablespoon fresh sage leaves, chopped

1 bay leaf

Salt and freshly ground black pepper, to taste

4 cups vegetable broth

1 (15-ounce) can cannellini beans, rinsed and drained

3 cups fresh spinach

1 large carrot, peeled and spiralized with Blade C

2 cups day-old crusty whole grain bread, torn into 1-inch pieces

¼ cup Parmesan cheese, grated

Directions:

1. *In a large pan, heat oil on medium heat.*
2. *Add celery and onion and sauté for about 4-5 minutes.*
3. *Add garlic and sauté for about 1 minute.*
4. *Add tomatoes, fresh herbs, bay leaf, salt, black pepper and broth and bring to a boil on medium-high heat.*
5. *Stir in the beans and spinach.*
6. *Reduce the heat to low and simmer, covered for about 25 minutes.*
7. *Stir in carrot noodles and bread and simmer for about 5 minutes.*
8. *Remove from the heat and discard bay leaf.*
9. *Serve hot with the topping of Parmesan cheese.*

Ginger Sweet Potato & Chickpeas Soup

Time: 55 minutes

Servings: 4

Ingredients:

1 tablespoon coconut oil

2 teaspoons ground ginger

1 teaspoons hot smoked paprika

½ teaspoons ground cinnamon

½ teaspoons freshly grated nutmeg

2 medium onions

Salt, to taste

Pinch of saffron soaked in 2 tablespoons of hot water

1 (14-ounce) can whole tomatoes, crushed

1 (6-oince) can tomato paste

3 cups canned chickpeas, rinsed and drained

1 cup dried lentils, soaked for overnight and drained

3 lemon slices

5 cups water

1 medium sweet potato, peeled and spiralized with Blade C

½ cup fresh cilantro, chopped

½ cup fresh parsley, chopped

Freshly ground pepper, to taste

Directions:

1. Steep the saffron threads in 2 tablespoons of boiled water for about 10-15 minutes.

2. In a large pan, melt coconut oil on medium-high heat.

3. Add spies and sauté for about 1 minute.

4. Reduce the heat to medium.

5. Add onions and salt and cook for about 10 minutes, stirring occasionally.

6. Add the steeped saffron water, tomatoes, tomato paste, chickpeas, lentils, lemon slices and water and bring to a boil.

7. Reduce the heat to low and simmer, covered for about 15-25 minutes or till desired doneness.

8. Add the sweet potato noodles and simmer for about 5 minutes.

9. Season with salt and black pepper and serve hot.

Carrots Zucchini & Bacon Soup

Time: 45 minutes

Servings: 6

Ingredients:

4 bacon strips

1 small onion, chopped

1 large carrot, peeled and chopped

1 celery stalk, chopped

2 garlic cloves, minced

1 tablespoon tomato paste

4 cups chicken broth

1 cup water

1 teaspoon fresh thyme

1 bay leaf

1 (14½-ounce) can chickpeas, rinsed and drained

1 large zucchini, spiralized with Blade C

¼ cup fresh parsley, chopped

Directions:

1. Heat a large skillet on medium-high heat.
2. Add bacon and cook for about 8-10 minutes or till crisp.
3. Transfer the bacon onto a paper towel lined plate to drain and then crumble it.
4. Transfer the bacon grease into a bowl and reserve.
5. In a large pan, heat 1 tablespoon of the reserved bacon grease on medium-high heat.
6. Add onion, celery and carrots and sauté for about 3 minutes.
7. Add garlic and sauté for about 30 seconds.
8. Stir in tomato paste, broth, water, remaining bacon grease, thyme and bay leaf and bring to a boil.
9. Add chickpeas and zucchini noodles and cook for about 5 minutes.
10. Remove from the heat and discard bay leaf.
11. Serve hot with the topping of the bacon and parsley.

Garlic Mixed Veggies & Bacon Soup

Time: 65 minutes

Servings: 6

Ingredients:

5 tablespoons olive oil, divided

4-ounces bacon slices, cut into ¼-inch pieces

1 large red onion, sliced thinly

3 garlic cloves, minced

1 tablespoon fresh basil, chopped finely

1 tablespoon fresh thyme, chopped finely

1 bay leaf

12 cups chicken broth

1 large carrot, peeled, spiralized with Blade C

1 large parsnip, peeled and spiralized with Blade C

1 medium turnip, peeled and spiralized with Blade C

8-ounce Brussels sprouts, trimmed and sliced thinly

Salt and freshly ground black pepper, to taste

2 teaspoons fresh lemon zest, grated finely

Directions:

1. Heat a large skillet on medium-high heat.

2. Add bacon and cook for about 8-10 minutes or till crisp.

3. Transfer the bacon onto a paper towel lined plate to drain and then crumble it.

4. Transfer 2 tablespoons of the bacon grease into a large pan on medium heat.

5. Add onion and cook for about 8-10 minutes, stirring occasionally.

6. Add garlic and sauté for about 1 minute.

7. Add bacon, basil, thyme, bay leaf and broth and bring to a boil.

8. Cook for about 15 minutes.

9. Add veggie noodles, Brussels sprouts, salt and black pepper and cook for about 3-4 minutes.

10. Remove from heat and discard bay leaves.

11. Serve hot with the topping of lemon zest.

Coconut Curried Zucchini Chicken Soup

Time: 30 minutes

Servings: 8

Ingredients:

1 tablespoon coconut oil

1 onion, chopped

2 garlic cloves, minced

1 jalapeño pepper, chopped

1½ tablespoons green curry paste

1 pound skinless, boneless chicken breasts, sliced thinly

6 cups chicken broth

1 (15-ounce) can full-fat coconut milk

1 red bell pepper, seeded and sliced thinly

2 tablespoons fish sauce

½ cup fresh cilantro, chopped

2 medium zucchinis, spiralized with Blade C

2 tablespoons fresh lime juice

Directions:

1. In a large pan, melt coconut oil on medium heat.
2. Add onion, carrots and mushrooms and sauté for 4-5 minutes.
3. Add garlic, jalapeño and curry paste and sauté for about 1 minute.
4. Add chicken and cook for about 3-4 minutes.
5. Stir in chicken broth and coconut milk and bring to a boil.
6. Stir in red pepper and fish sauce.
7. Reduce the heat to medium-low and simmer for about 5 minutes.
8. Stir in cilantro and remove from heat.
9. Divide zucchini noodles in serving bowls.
10. Pour hot soup over noodles.
11. Serve hot with the drizzling of lime juice.

Jalapeno Zucchini, Salsa & Chicken Soup

Time: 25 minutes

Servings: 4

Ingredients:

4 cups chicken broth

2 cooked chicken breasts, diced or shredded

3 tablespoon prepared salsa

1 jalapeño pepper, sliced

1 teaspoon garlic powder

1 teaspoon red chili powder

½ teaspoon ground cumin

Salt and freshly ground black pepper, to taste

1 tablespoon fresh lime juice

1 large zucchini, spiralized with Blade C

1 large avocado, peeled, pitted and chopped

Directions:

1. In a large pan, add broth on high heat and bring to a boil.

2. Reduce the heat to medium-low.

3. Stir in remaining ingredients except zucchini and avocado and cook for about 2 minutes.

4. Add zucchini noodles and cook for about 2-3 minutes.

5. Serve hot with the topping of avocado.

Mushroom Zucchini, Yellow Squash & Chicken Soup

Time: 65 minutes

Servings: 4

Ingredients:

2 tablespoons extra-virgin olive oil

1 medium white onion, chopped

2 medium carrots, peeled and chopped

1½ cups Portobello mushrooms, chopped

1 teaspoon dried oregano, crushed

½ teaspoon ground cumin

½ teaspoon cayenne pepper

5 cups chicken broth

3 cups cooked chicken, shredded

1 medium zucchinis, spiralized with Blade C

1 medium yellow squash, spiralized with Blade C

Salt and freshly ground black pepper, to taste

2 tablespoons fresh lime juice

¼ cup fresh parsley leaves, chopped

Directions:

1. *In a large pan, heat oil on medium heat.*
2. *Add onion, carrots and mushrooms and sauté for 4-5 minutes.*

3. Add thyme and spices and sauté for about 1 minute.

4. Add chicken and broth and bring to a boil.

5. Reduce the heat to low and simmer for about 30-35 minutes.

6. Stir in zucchini, salt and black pepper and cook for about 3-4 minutes.

7. Stir in lemon juice and parsley and immediately remove from heat.

8. Serve hot.

Carrots Yellow Squash & Chicken Soup

Time: 55 minutes

Servings: 4

Ingredients:

2 tablespoons extra virgin olive oil

1 medium white onion, chopped

2 cups celery stalks, chopped

3 cups carrots, peeled and chopped

3 garlic cloves, minced

7-8 cups chicken broth

3 large yellow squash, spiralized with Blade C

2 grass fed cooked skinless, boneless chicken breasts, shredded

Salt and freshly ground black pepper, to taste

Directions:

1. In a large pan, heat oil on medium heat.
2. Add onion, celery and carrots and sauté for 4-5 minutes.
3. Add garlic and sauté for 1 minute.
4. Add broth and bring to a boil.
5. Reduce the heat to low and simmer, covered for about 20-25 minutes.
6. Stir in spiralized squash and chicken and cook for 2-3 minutes.
7. Season with salt and pepper and remove from heat.
8. Serve hot.

Basil Carrot & Chicken Soup

Time: 35 minutes

Servings: 4

Ingredients:

2 tablespoon olive oil

½ medium red onion, chopped

2 celery stalks, chopped

2 garlic cloves, minced

Salt and freshly ground black pepper, to taste

½ teaspoon dried basil, crushed

½ teaspoon dried oregano, crushed

4 cups chicken broth

2 cups cooked chicken, shredded

1 large carrot, peeled and spiralized with Blade C

Directions:

1. In a large pan, heat oil on medium heat.
2. Add onion, celery, garlic, salt and black pepper and sauté for about 4-5 minutes.
3. Add broth and bring to a boil on high heat.
4. Add broth and herbs and bring to a boil.
5. Reduce the heat to low and cook for about 5-7 minutes.
6. Add chicken and carrot noodles and cook for about 5 minutes.
7. Serve hot.

Celery Carrot & Chicken Soup

Time: 50 minutes

Servings: 2

Ingredients:

1 tablespoon extra-virgin olive oil

1/3 cup onion, chopped

1 celery stalk, chopped

2 teaspoons garlic, minced

½ of jalapeño pepper, seeded and chopped

1 teaspoon red chili powder

1¾ cups tomatoes, chopped finely

1 teaspoon dried rosemary, crushed

3 cups chicken broth

Salt and freshly ground black pepper, to taste

3 medium carrots, peeled and spiralized with Blade C

1 cooked skinless, boneless chicken breast, shredded

1 tablespoon fresh lemon juice

1 tablespoon fresh parsley, chopped

Directions:

1. In a large pan, heat oil on medium heat.

2. Add onion and sauté for about 4-5 minutes.

3. Add garlic, jalapeño, rosemary and chili powder and sauté for about 1 minute.

4. Add tomatoes and thyme and cook for about 3 to 4 minutes.

5. Add broth, salt and black pepper and bring to a boil.

6. Reduce the heat to low and simmer, covered for about 15-20 minutes.

7. Stir in carrot and chicken and cook for 5 minutes.

8. Stir in lemon juice and parsley and remove from heat.

9. Serve hot.

Cilantro Curried Turnip & Chicken Soup

Time: 55 minutes

Servings: 3

Ingredients:

6 cups water

2 cups of water

1 (12-ounce) chicken breast (with bones), skin discarded

2 teaspoons red curry paste

2 large turnips, peeled and spiralized with Blade C

1 red bell pepper, seeded and sliced thinly

5 scallions, chopped

Salt and freshly ground black pepper, to taste

¼ cup fresh cilantro leaves

1 lime, cut into wedges

Directions:

1. In a large pan, add water on medium heat and bring to a boil.

2. Reduce the heat to low and simmer, covered for about 30 minutes.

3. Remove the chicken and keep aside to cool and then shred it.

4. In the pan of broth, add curry paste and stir to combine.

5. Bring to a boil on medium-high heat.

6. Add the turnip noodles and bell pepper and cook for about 3 minutes.

7. Stir in the shredded chicken, scallions, salt and black pepper and cook for about 2-3 minutes.

8. Stir in cilantro and remove from heat.

9. Serve hot with the lime wedges.

Rosemary Rutabaga & Turkey Soup

Time: 35 minutes

Servings: 6

Ingredients:

1 tablespoon olive oil

2 large carrots, peeled and chopped

1 large onion, chopped

1 large scallion, chopped finely

6 garlic cloves, minced

1½ teaspoons dried thyme, crushed

1½ teaspoons dried rosemary, crushed

1½ teaspoons dried oregano, crushed

2 teaspoons hot paprika

Salt and freshly ground black pepper, to taste

6 cups chicken broth

2 cups cooked turkey, shredded

2 cups fresh kale, trimmed and chopped

1 small rutabaga, peeled and spiralized with Blade C

Directions:

1. In a large pan, heat oil on medium heat.

2. Add carrots, onion, scallion and garlic and sauté for about 5-7 minutes.

3. Add garlic, herbs and seasonings and sauté for about 1 minute.

4. Add broth and bring to a boil.

5. Add turkey, kale and rutabaga noodles and cook for about 10 minutes. Serve hot.

Delicious Zucchini & Turkey Soup

Time: 65 minutes

Servings: 6

Ingredients:

1 tablespoon extra-virgin olive oil

1 small yellow onion, chopped

1 cup carrots, peeled and chopped

1 cup celery stalk, chopped

1 garlic clove, minced

6 cups chicken broth

1 pound cooked turkey breast, chopped

1 teaspoon fresh parsley, chopped

½ teaspoon dried oregano, crushed

3 bay leaves

2 cups Zucchini, spiralized with Blade C

Salt and freshly ground black pepper, to taste

Directions:

1. In a large pan, heat oil on medium heat.

2. Add onion, carrot, celery and garlic and sauté for about 4-5 minutes.

3. Add remaining ingredients except zucchini and bring to a boil.

4. Reduce heat to low and simmer, covered for about 15 minutes.

5. Add zucchini noodles and cook for about 2-3 minutes.

6. Season with salt and pepper and remove from heat.

7. Discard bay leaf and serve hot.

Sesame Oil Zucchini, Seaweed & Turkey Soup

Time: 25 minutes

Servings: 4

Ingredients:

4 cups vegetable broth

1 cup cooked turkey, cut into small pieces

2 cups fresh kale, trimmed and chopped

1 cup fresh shiitake mushrooms, sliced

2 tablespoons dry seaweed

1 (2-inche) piece fresh ginger, sliced thinly

2 garlic cloves, minced

Salt and freshly ground black pepper, to taste

2 medium zucchinis, spiralized with Blade C

2 teaspoons sesame oil, toasted

Directions:

1. In a large pan, add broth on medium heat and bring to a boil.

2. Add turkey, kale, mushrooms, seaweed, ginger, garlic, salt and black pepper and bring to a boil.

3. Reduce the heat and simmer, covered for about 3-4 minutes.

4. Add zucchini noodles and simmer for about 2-3 minutes.

5. Remove from heat.

6. Stir in sesame oil and serve.

Cumin Yellow Squash & Turkey Meatballs Soup

Time: 55 minutes

Servings: 4

Ingredients:

For Meatballs:

¾ pound lean ground turkey

1 medium egg, beaten

½ teaspoon ground cumin

Salt and freshly ground black pepper, to taste

For Soup:

1 tablespoon extra-virgin coconut oil

1 small yellow onion, chopped

2 small carrots, peeled and chopped

3 stalks celery, chopped

3-4 garlic cloves, minced

½ teaspoon dried rosemary, crushed

½ teaspoon dried basil, crushed

½ teaspoon ground cumin

¼ teaspoon red pepper flakes, crushed

¼ teaspoon cayenne pepper

5 cups chicken broth

1 large fresh tomato, chopped finely

2 medium yellow squash, spiralized with Blade C

Salt and freshly ground black pepper, to taste

¼ cup fresh cilantro leaves, chopped

1 avocado, peeled, pitted and chopped

Directions:

1. *In a large bowl, add all meatballs ingredients and mix till well combined.*
2. *Make desired size meatballs from mixture and keep aside.*
3. *In a large pan, heat oil on medium heat.*
4. *Add onion, carrots and celery and sauté for 6-8 minutes.*
5. *Add garlic, herbs and spices and sauté for about 1 minute.*
6. *Add tomatoes and cook for 1-2 minutes.*
7. *Add broth and bring to a boil.*
8. *Cook for about 5 minutes.*
9. *Stir in meatballs.*
10. *Reduce the heat to low and simmer for about 15 minutes.*
11. *Stir in squash, salt and black pepper and cook for about 3-4 minutes.*
12. *Stir in cilantro and immediately remove from heat.*
13. *Garnish with avocado and serve hot.*

Mushroom Yellow Squash & Beef Soup

Time: 45 minutes

Servings: 2

Ingredients:

1½ tablespoons extra virgin olive oil, divided

½ pound New York strip steak, cut into bite sized pieces

Salt and freshly ground black pepper, to taste

1 small onion, chopped

3-4 garlic cloves, minced

1 cup shiitake mushrooms, chopped

1 cup fresh spinach, torn

3½ cups beef broth

2 tablespoons tamari

1 large yellow squash, spiralized with Blade C

½ cup scallion, chopped

Directions:

1. In a large pan, heat 1 tablespoon of oil on medium heat.
2. Add beef and sprinkle with salt and black pepper.
3. Cook for about 6-8 minutes or till golden brown from all sides.
4. Transfer the beef into a bowl.
5. In the same pan, heat remaining oil on medium heat.

6. Add onion and sauté for about 4-5 minutes.

7. Add garlic and sauté for about 1 minute.

8. Add mushrooms and cook for about 3-4 minutes. Add spinach and cook for about 2 to 3 minutes.

9. Add beef broth and tamari and bring to a boil.

10. Reduce the heat to medium-low and simmer for about 10-15 minutes.

11. Stir in squash, scallion, salt and black pepper and simmer for about 2-3 minutes.

12. Remove from heat and serve hot.

Ground Beef Soup & Zucchini

Time: 55 minutes

Servings: 4

Ingredients:

1 tablespoon extra-virgin olive oil

¼ cup white onion, chopped

2 celery stalks, chopped

½ cup green bell pepper, seeded and chopped

½ pound ground beef

3 cups fresh tomatoes, chopped finely

4 cups beef broth

1 tablespoon fresh thyme, minced

3 medium zucchinis, spiralized with Blade C

Salt and freshly ground black pepper, to taste

1 tablespoon fresh lemon juice

½ cup scallions, chopped

Directions:

1. In a large pan, heat oil on medium heat.
2. Add onion, celery and bell pepper and sauté for about 4-5 minutes.
3. Add beef and cook for 4-5 minutes.
4. Add tomatoes and cook for 1-2 minutes.
5. Add broth and thyme and bring to a boil.
6. Reduce the heat to low and simmer, covered for about 20-25 minutes.
7. Stir in zucchini, scallion, salt and black pepper and simmer for about 2-3 minutes.
8. Stir in lemon juice and remove from heat.
9. Garnish with scallion and serve hot.

Black Olive Zucchini & Meatballs Soup

Time: 50 minutes

Servings: 2

Ingredients:

For Meatballs:

1 pound extra lean ground beef

½ red onion, chopped

4-6 black olives, pitted and chopped

1 small red bell pepper, seeded and chopped

3 garlic cloves, chopped finely

2 tablespoons fresh parsley, chopped

¼ cup coconut flour

1 egg, beaten

½ teaspoon cayenne pepper

Salt and freshly ground black pepper, to taste

1 tablespoon extra-virgin olive oil

For Soup:

2 tablespoons extra-virgin olive oil

1 medium onion, chopped

2 celery stalks, chopped

1 carrot, peeled and chopped finely

2 garlic cloves, minced

7-8 cups beef broth

1½ cups fresh kale, trimmed and chopped

1 teaspoon dried oregano, crushed

Salt and freshly ground black pepper, to taste

2-3 large zucchinis, spiralized with Blade C

1 tablespoon fresh lemon juice

Directions:

1. For meatballs in a large bowl, add all ingredients except oil and mix till well combined.

2. Make desired size balls from mixture.

3. In a large skillet, heat oil on medium heat.

4. Add meatballs in batches and cook for about 3-4 minutes or till golden brown from all sides.

5. Transfer the meatballs into a plate and keep aside.

6. In a large pan, heat oil on medium heat.

7. Add onion, celery and carrot and sauté for about 4-5 minutes.

8. Add garlic and sauté for about 1 minute.

9. Add broth and bring to a boil.

10. Reduce the heat to medium-low and simmer for about 3-4 minutes.

11. Carefully, add in the meatballs and simmer, covered for about 10 minutes.

12. Stir in kale, oregano, salt and black pepper and cook for about 2-3 minutes.

13. Stir in zucchini and cook for about 23 minutes.

14. Stir in lemon juice and remove from heat.

15. Serve hot.

Ginger Zucchini & Lamb Soup

Time: 1 hour 50 minutes

Servings: 4

Ingredients:

2 tablespoons extra-virgin olive oil

2 large lamb shanks

1 medium yellow onion, chopped

2 celery stalks, chopped

2 small carrots, peeled and chopped

2 garlic cloves, minced

1 teaspoon fresh ginger, minced

½ teaspoon dried oregano, crushed

½ teaspoon dried thyme, crushed

1 teaspoon ground coriander

1½ teaspoons ground cumin

1 teaspoon cayenne pepper

2 cups tomatoes, chopped

6 cups chicken broth

3 medium zucchinis, spiralized with Blade C

Salt and freshly ground black pepper, to taste

½ cup fresh parsley, chopped

Directions:

1. In a large pan, heat oil on medium heat.
2. Add shanks and cook for 6-8 minutes or till browned from all sides.
3. Transfer the shanks into a bowl.
4. In the same pan, add onion, celery and carrot and sauté for about 4-5 minutes.
5. Add garlic, ginger, herbs and spices and sauté for about 1 minute.
6. Add tomatoes and cook for about 1-2 minutes.
7. Add cooked shanks and broth and bring to a boil.
8. Reduce the heat to low and simmer, covered partially for about 1½ hours.
9. Remove shanks from soup and shred the meat.
10. Stir in shredded meat, zucchini, salt and black pepper and simmer for about 3-4 minutes.
11. Garnish with parsley and serve hot.

Garlic Sweet Potato & Ground Pork Soup

Time: 45 minutes

Servings: 4

Ingredients:

1 tablespoon olive oil

1 teaspoon fresh ginger, minced

2 garlic cloves, minced

½ teaspoon dried thyme, crushed

½ teaspoon ground cumin

¼ teaspoon ground coriander

½ teaspoon red pepper flakes, crushed

1 pound lean ground pork

Salt and freshly ground black pepper, to taste

4 cups chicken broth

1 medium sweet potato, peeled and spiralized with Blade C

4 cups fresh spinach, torn

1 cup scallion, chopped

Directions:

1. In a large pan, heat oil on medium heat.
2. Add ginger, garlic, thyme and spices and sauté for about 1 minute.
3. Add pork and sprinkle with salt and black pepper.
4. Cook for about 9-10 minutes, stirring and breaking with a spoon.

5. Add broth and bring to a boil.
6. Reduce the heat to low and simmer for about 8-10 minutes.
7. Add sweet potato and simmer for about 5 minutes.
8. Add spinach and scallion and simmer for about 3-4 minutes.
9. Season with salt and black pepper and serve hot.

Cilantro Ginger Radish & Pork Meatballs Soup

Time: 55 minutes

Servings: 4

Ingredients:

For Meatballs:

1 pound lean ground pork

1/3 cup scallions, chopped

3 teaspoons fresh cilantro, chopped

1 teaspoon garlic, minced

1 teaspoon fresh ginger, minced

1 tablespoon soy sauce

Salt and freshly ground black pepper, to taste

For Soup:

1 teaspoon sesame oil

1 tablespoon fresh ginger, minced

2 bunches broccolini, trimmed and halved

Freshly ground black pepper, to taste

4 cups chicken broth

2 cups water

1 tablespoon fish sauce

1 tablespoon soy sauce

2 teaspoons Sriracha

3 medium daikon radishes, peeled and spiralized with Blade C

½ cup fresh cilantro leaves, chopped

Directions:

1. Preheat the oven to 400 degrees F.
2. Line a baking sheet with a parchment paper.
3. For meatballs in a large bowl, add all ingredients and mix till well combined.
4. Make about 10-12 golf ball sized meatballs from the mixture.
5. Arrange the balls onto prepared baking sheet in a single layer.
6. Bake for about 18 minutes.
7. Meanwhile in a large pan, heat oil on medium heat.
8. Add ginger and sauté for about 1 minute.
9. Add broccolini and pepper and cook for about 3-5 minutes.
10. Add broth, water, fish sauce, soy sauce and Sriracha and bring to a boil.
11. Reduce the heat to low and simmer for about 10 minutes.
12. Add radish noodles and cook for about 3-5 minutes.
13. Divide the soup into serving bowls and top with meatballs.
14. Serve hot with the garnishing of cilantro.

Onion Carrot & Sausage Soup

Time: 40 minutes

Servings: 4

Ingredients:

¾ pound sweet Italian sausage, casing removed

½ cup onion, chopped

2 garlic cloves, minced

Salt and freshly ground black pepper, to taste

4 cups curly kale, chopped

6 cups chicken broth

1 teaspoon dried oregano, crushed

1 large carrot, peeled and spiralized with Blade C

1 teaspoon red pepper flakes, crushed

¼ cup Parmesan cheese, shredded

Directions:

1. Heat a large pan on medium-high heat.
2. Add sausage and cook for about 10-15 minutes, crumbling with a wooden spoon.
3. Add onion, garlic, salt and black pepper and cook for about 3 minutes.
4. Add kale and cook for about 1 minute.
5. Add broth and oregano and bring to a boil on high heat.
6. Stir in carrot noodles.

7. Reduce the heat to low and simmer for about 5 minutes.

8. Stir in red pepper flakes and remove from heat.

9. Serve hot with the topping of Parmesan cheese.

Pesto Zucchini & Sausage Soup

Time: 40 minutes

Servings: 4

Ingredients:

For Soup:

1 tablespoon extra-virgin olive oil

4 chicken sausage links, casing removed

2 celery stalks, chopped

½ of red onion, chopped

2 garlic cloves, minced

¼ teaspoon red pepper flakes

Salt and freshly ground black pepper, to taste

6 cups chicken broth

2 medium zucchinis, spiralized with Blade C

For Pesto:

2 cups fresh basil

1 large garlic clove, chopped

2 tablespoons parmesan cheese

1 tablespoon pine nuts

1 tablespoon extra-virgin olive oil

Salt and freshly ground black pepper, to taste

Directions:

1. In a large pan, heat oil on medium-high heat.
2. Add sausage and cook for about 5 minutes, crumbling with a wooden spoon.
3. Add in celery, onion, garlic, red pepper flakes, salt and black pepper and cook for about 3 minutes.
4. Add broth and bring to a boil.
5. Cook for about 5 minutes.
6. Add zucchini noodles and cook for about 3-4 minutes.
7. Meanwhile for pesto in a food processor, add all ingredients and pulse till smooth.
8. Add the pesto in the soup and stir to combine.
9. Serve immediately.

Tasty Salmon Fillets Soup & Zucchini

Time: 30 minutes

Servings: 2

Ingredients:

2 (3-ounce) salmon fillets

Salt and freshly ground black pepper, to taste

1 tablespoon extra-virgin olive oil

2 garlic cloves, minced

1 teaspoon fresh ginger, minced

1½ cups fresh spinach, torn

2 cups fish broth

2 tablespoons soy sauce

2 medium zucchinis, spiralized with Blade C

¼ cup scallions, chopped

Directions:

1. Arrange a steamer basket over a pan of boiling water.

2. In steamer basket, place the salmon fillets and sprinkle with salt and black pepper.

3. Steam, covered for about 5-6 minutes.

4. Meanwhile in a large skillet, heat oil on medium heat.

5. Add garlic and ginger and sauté for about 1 minute.

6. Add spinach and cook for about 2-3 minutes.

7. Add broth and soy sauce and bring to a boil.

8. Stir in zucchini, salt and black pepper and cook for about 4-5 minutes.

9. Sir in salmon and scallion and remove from heat. Serve hot.

Jalapeno Zucchini & Herring Soup

Time: 25 minutes

Servings: 2

Ingredients:

1 tablespoon extra-virgin olive oil

1 teaspoon fresh ginger, grated finely

2 (3-ounce) herring fillets

Salt and freshly ground black pepper, to taste

2 cups chicken broth

1 small jalapeño pepper, seeded and minced

2 medium zucchinis, spiralized with Blade C

¼ cup scallion, chopped

1 tablespoon fresh lemon juice

¼ teaspoon fresh lemon zest, grated finely

Directions:

1. In a large skillet, heat oil on medium-high heat.
2. Add ginger and sauté for about 30 seconds.
3. Add herring and sprinkle with salt and black pepper and cook for about 8 minutes, flipping once in the middle way.
4. Meanwhile in a large pan, add broth and bring to boil on high heat.
5. Reduce the heat to medium.
6. Stir in jalapeño pepper and zucchini and cook for about 2-3 minutes.
7. Stir in cooked herring, scallion, lemon juice, salt and black pepper and remove from heat.
8. Top with lemon zest and serve hot.

Ginger Zucchini & Shrimp Soup

Time: 25 minutes

Servings: 4

Ingredients:

2 cups chicken broth

1¾ cups unsweetened coconut milk

½ teaspoon fresh ginger, grated

1 pound shrimp, peeled and deveined

1 large zucchini, spiralized with Blade C

2 tablespoons fresh lime juice

Salt and freshly ground black pepper, to taste

3 tablespoons fresh cilantro leaves, chopped

Directions:

1. In a large pan, add broth and coconut milk and bring to a boil on medium-high heat.

2. Reduce the heat to medium-low.

3. Add shrimp and zucchini and cook for 4-5 minutes.

4. Stir in lime juice, salt and black pepper and remove from heat.

5. Garnish with cilantro and serve hot.

Nutritious Mixed Veggie Stew

Time: 60 minutes

Servings: 4

Ingredients:

2 tablespoons olive oil

1 yellow onion, chopped

2 large garlic cloves, minced

¼ teaspoon red pepper flakes, crushed

1 medium zucchini, spiralized with Blade C

1 medium yellow squash, spiralized with Blade C

2 red bell peppers, seeded and sliced thinly

1 cup eggplant, julienned

Salt and freshly ground black pepper, to taste

1 (28-ounce) can whole peeled tomatoes with juice

1 tablespoon fresh oregano, chopped

½ cup vegetable broth

1 bay leaf

¼ cup fresh basil, chopped

Directions:

1. In a large pan, heat oil on medium heat.

2. Add onion, garlic and red pepper flakes and sauté for about 4-5 minutes.

3. Add zucchini, squash, bell pepper, eggplant, salt and black pepper and cook for about 7-10 minutes.

4. With your hands, crush the tomatoes in the pan.

5. Stir in tomato juice from can, oregano, bay leaf and bring to a boil on high heat.

6. Reduce the heat to low and simmer for about 10-15 minutes.

7. Stir in basil and cook for about 1 minute.

8. Discard the bay leaf and serve hot.

Garlic Onion Rutabaga & Beans Stew

Time: 60 minutes

Servings: 4

Ingredients:

1 large rutabaga, peeled and spiralized with Blade C

2½ tablespoons olive oil, divided

Salt and freshly ground black pepper, to taste

1 cup celery stalk, chopped

1 cup carrot, peeled and chopped

½ cup white onion, chopped

4 garlic cloves, minced

1 teaspoon dried basil, crushed

1 teaspoon dried oregano, crushed

½ teaspoon cayenne pepper

½ teaspoon ground cumin

3 cups fresh spinach, torn

3 cups vegetable broth

2 cups tomatoes, chopped

1½ cups canned navy beans, rinsed and drained

2 tablespoons fresh lemon juice

Directions:

1. Preheat the oven to 425 degrees F.
2. Line a baking dish with parchment paper.
3. In a bowl, add rutabaga noodles, 1 tablespoon of oil, salt and black pepper and toss to coat well.
4. Arrange the rutabaga noodles onto the prepared baking dish.
5. Bake for about 15-20 minutes.
6. Meanwhile in a large pan, heat remaining oil on medium heat.
7. Add celery, carrot and onion and sauté for about 5-7 minutes.
8. Add garlic, herbs and spices and sauté for about 1 minute.
9. Add spinach and cook for about 1-2 minutes.
10. Add broth, tomatoes and beans and bring to a boil.
11. Reduce the heat to low and simmer for about 20-30 minutes.
12. Stir in lemon juice, salt and black pepper and remove from heat.
13. Divide the rutabaga noodles in 4 serving bowls.
14. Pour stew over rutabaga noodles evenly and serve.

Cumin Thyme Butternut Squash & Beans Stew

Time: 50 minutes

Servings: 6

Ingredients:

1 tablespoon extra-virgin olive oil

1 onion, chopped

1 celery stalk, chopped

1 carrot, peeled and chopped

2 garlic cloves, minced

1 Serrano pepper, seeded and chopped

½ teaspoon dried thyme, crushed

½ teaspoon dried basil, crushed

½ teaspoon ground cumin

½ teaspoon smoked paprika

1 (15-ounce) can diced tomatoes with juice

5 cups vegetable broth

1 butternut squash, peeled and spiralized with Blade C

3 cups fresh spinach, trimmed and chopped

1 cup canned navy beans, rinsed and drained

¼ cup scallion, chopped

Salt and freshly ground black pepper, to taste

2 tablespoons fresh lemon juice

Directions:

1. In a large pan, heat oil on medium heat.

2. Add onions, celery and carrot and sauté for about 4-5 minutes.

3. Add garlic, Serrano pepper, herbs and spices and sauté for about 1 minute.

4. Add tomatoes and cook, crushing with the back of a wooden spoon.

5. Add broth and bring to a boil.

6. Stir in squash and beans and reduce the heat to low.

7. Simmer, covered for about 15 minutes.

8. Stir in spinach and scallion and simmer for about 5 minutes.

9. Stir in salt, black pepper and lemon juice and remove from heat.

10. Serve hot.

Yummy Zucchini & Chicken Stew

Time: 65 minutes

Servings: 4

Ingredients:

2½ tablespoons olive oil, divided

2½ pound boneless chicken, cubed

Salt and freshly ground black pepper, to taste

1 large carrot, peeled and sliced thinly

1 large white onion, chopped

1 medium red bell pepper, seeded and cut into thin strips

1 medium orange bell pepper, seeded and cut into thin strips

2 garlic cloves, minced

2 Serrano pepper, seeded and chopped

2 cups fresh tomatoes, chopped finely

2 cups chicken broth

2 large zucchinis, spiralized with Blade C

¼ cup fresh cilantro leaves, chopped

Directions:

1. In a large pan, heat 2 tablespoons of oil on medium heat.
2. Add chicken and sprinkle with salt and black pepper and cook for about 8-10 minutes.
3. Transfer the chicken into a large plate.
4. In the same pan, add carrot, onion and bell peppers and sauté for about 3-4 minutes.
5. Add garlic and Serrano pepper and sauté for about 1 minute.
6. Add tomatoes and cook for about 1-2 minutes, crushing with the back of a wooden spoon.
7. Add broth and chicken and bring to a boil.
8. Reduce the heat to low and simmer for about 20-25 minutes.
9. Add zucchini, salt and black pepper and cook for about 23 minutes.
10. Stir in cilantro, salt and black pepper and remove from heat.
11. Serve hot.

Celery Rutabaga & Beef Stew

Time: 2 hours 15 minutes

Servings: 4

Ingredients:

1 tablespoon extra-virgin coconut oil

1 pound beef stew meat, trimmed and cubed

Salt and freshly ground black pepper, to taste

2 celery stalks, chopped

1 large onion, chopped

2 garlic cloves, minced

10-12 fresh tomatoes, chopped finely

½ cup tomato puree

2½ cups water

1 teaspoon dried oregano, crushed

1 teaspoon dried thyme, crushed

½ teaspoon cayenne pepper

6 small rutabagas, peeled and spiralized with Blade C

Directions:

1. In a large pan, heat oil on medium-high-heat.

2. Add beef and sprinkle with salt and black pepper and cook for about 4-5 minutes or till browned from all sides.

3. Transfer the beef into a plate.

4. In the same pan, add celery and onion and sauté for 4-5 minutes.

5. Add garlic and sauté for about 1 minute.

6. Add tomatoes and cook for about 1-2 minutes, crushing with the back of a wooden spoon.

7. Add beef and remaining ingredients except rutabaga noodles and bring to a boil.

8. Reduce the heat to low and simmer, covered for about 2 hours.

9. Meanwhile, arrange a steamer basket in a pan of boiling water.

10. Place the rutabaga noodles in steamer basket and sprinkle with salt.

11. Steam, covered for about 4-5 minutes.

12. Divide rutabaga noodles into serving bowls and top with beef mixture and serve.

Garlic Tamari Zucchini, Squash & Beef Stew

Time: 1 hour 30 minutes

Servings: 4

Ingredients:

½ tablespoon olive oil

1 pound beef stew meat, cubed

Salt and freshly ground black pepper, to taste

1 medium onion, chopped

4 celery stalks, chopped

2 large carrots, peeled and chopped

2 garlic cloves, minced

1 Serrano pepper, chopped

2 bay leaves

1 teaspoon dried thyme, crushed

1 teaspoon ground coriander

2 teaspoons ground cumin

½ teaspoon cayenne pepper

2 cups tomatoes, chopped finely

5 cups chicken broth

2 tablespoons tamari

2 large zucchinis, spiralized with Blade C

2 yellow squash, spiralized with Blade C

½ cup fresh cilantro, chopped

Directions:

1. In a large pan, heat oil on medium heat.

2. Add beef and sprinkle with salt and black pepper and cook for about 4-5 minutes or till browned from all sides.

3. Transfer the beef into a bowl.

4. In the same pan, add onion, celery and carrots and sauté for about 4-5 minutes.

5. Add garlic, Serrano pepper, bay leaves, thyme and spices and sauté for about 1 minute.

6. Add tomatoes and cook for about 2-3 minutes.

7. Add beef, broth and tamari and bring to a boil.

8. Reduce the heat to low and simmer, covered partially for about 40 minutes.

9. Uncover and simmer for about 25-30 minutes.

10. Stir in zucchini, squash, salt and black pepper and cook for about 4-5 minutes. Garnish with cilantro and serve hot.

Parsley Zucchini & Lamb Stew

Time: 1 hour 50 minutes

Servings: 4

Ingredients:

2 tablespoons canola oil, divided

1 pound lamb stew meat, trimmed and cubed

Salt and freshly ground black pepper, to taste

1 small onion, chopped

2 carrots, peeled and chopped

2 celery stalks, chopped

2 garlic cloves, minced

1 (15-ounce) can diced tomatoes

½ tablespoon smoked paprika

3 cups chicken broth

2 tablespoons tomato paste

4 medium zucchinis, spiralized with Blade C

2 tablespoons fresh lemon juice

¼ cups fresh parsley leaves, chopped

Directions:

1. In a large pan, heat oil on medium heat.
2. Add lamb and sprinkle with salt and black pepper and cook for about 4-5 minutes or till browned completely.
3. Transfer the lamb into a bowl.
4. In the same pan, heat remaining oil on medium heat.
5. Add onion, carrots and celery and sauté for about 5-6 minutes.
6. Add garlic and sauté for about 1 minute.
7. Add tomatoes and paprika and cook for about 2-3 minutes, crushing with the back of spoon.
8. Add lamb, broth and tomato paste and bring to a boil on high heat.
9. Reduce the heat to low and simmer, covered for about 1½ hours or till desired thickness.
10. Uncover and stir in zucchini and cook for about 4-5 minutes.
11. Stir in lemon juice, salt and black pepper and remove from heat.
12. Garnish with parsley and serve.

Garlic Rosemary Potato & Cod Stew

Time: 50 minutes

Servings: 6

Ingredients:

2 teaspoons olive oil

4 large carrots, peeled and chopped

1 large onion, chopped

3 garlic cloves, minced

½ teaspoon dried rosemary, crushed

Salt and freshly ground black pepper, to taste

4 cups chicken broth

2 pound potatoes, peeled and spiralized with Blade C

1 (15-ounce) can diced tomatoes with juice

1 (6-ounce) can tomato sauce

1 pound cod fillets

Directions:

1. In a large pan, heat oil on medium heat.

2. Add onion and carrots and cook, covered for about 6-8 minutes, stirring occasionally.

3. Add garlic, rosemary, salt and black pepper and sauté for about 1 minute.

4. Add broth and bring to a boil.

5. Reduce the heat to low and simmer, covered for about 8-10 minutes.

6. Stir in potato noodles, with juices and tomato sauce and bring to a gentle simmer. Simmer for about 4-5 minutes.

8. Stir in the cod and simmer for about 4-5 minutes. Serve

Kernels Zucchini & Shrimp Stew

Time: 50 minutes

Servings: 4

Ingredients:

2 tablespoons olive oil

1 large onion, chopped

2 garlic cloves, minced

2 poblano peppers, seeded and chopped

Salt and freshly ground black pepper, to taste

1 (28-ounce) can diced tomatoes with juice

2 cups fish broth

1 pound medium shrimp, peeled and deveined

1 large zucchini, spiralized with Blade C

2 cups frozen corn kernels, thawed

Directions:

1. In a large pan, heat oil on medium-high heat.

2. Add onion, garlic, poblano peppers, salt and black pepper and cook for about 10-12 minutes, stirring occasionally.

3. Add the tomatoes with juice and cook and cook for about 10-12 minutes, stirring occasionally.

4. Add broth and bring to a boil on medium heat.

5. Add shrimp, zucchini and corn and simmer for about 5-6 minutes.

6. Serve hot.

CHAPTER 6 SPIRALIZER MEAT & SEAFOOD RECIPES

Zucchini with Spinach & Steak

Time: 35 minutes

Servings: 2

Ingredients:

¼ cup soy sauce

1 tablespoon balsamic vinegar

½ teaspoon red pepper flakes, crushed

2 tablespoons olive oil, divided

½ pound beef round steak, trimmed and cut into thin strips

Salt and freshly ground black pepper, to taste

¼ cup onion, chopped

1 garlic clove, minced

1 teaspoon fresh ginger, minced

1 jalapeño pepper, seeded and chopped

2 cups fresh spinach, chopped

2 medium zucchinis, spiralized with Blade C

2 tablespoons scallions, chopped

1 tablespoon black sesame seeds

Directions:

1. In a bowl, mix together soy sauce, vinegar and red pepper flakes and keep aside.

2. In a large skillet, heat 1 tablespoon of oil on medium heat.

3. Add steak strips and sprinkle with cayenne pepper, salt and black pepper and stir fry for about 3-4 minutes or till browned from all sides.

4. Transfer the steak strips into a bowl.

5. In the same skillet, heat remaining oil on medium heat.

6. Add onion and sauté for about 4-5 minutes.

7. Add garlic, ginger and jalapeño pepper and sauté for about 1 minute.

8. Add spinach and soy sauce mixture and cook for about 2 minutes.

9. Add zucchini and cook for about 2-3 minutes.

10. Stir in steak strips and scallion and remove from heat.

11. Garnish with sesame seeds and serve.

Coconut Zucchini Steak

Time: 40 minutes

Servings: 4

Ingredients:

1½ tablespoons olive oil, divided

1 pound skirt steak, trimmed and sliced thinly

Salt and freshly ground black pepper, to taste

½ teaspoon arrowroot powder

¼ cup vegetable broth

1 garlic clove, minced

1 cup coconut milk

½ teaspoon coconut aminos

3-4 zucchinis, spiralized with Blade C

2 tablespoons fresh parsley leaves, chopped

Directions:

1. In a large skillet, heat 1 tablespoon of oil on medium-high heat.

2. Add steak and sprinkle with salt and black pepper and cook the steak for about 5 minutes, flipping once in the middle way.

3. Transfer the steak into a late.

4. In the same skillet, heat remaining oil on medium heat.

5. Meanwhile in a bowl, mix together arrowroot and broth.

6. Add garlic in the preheated skillet and sauté for about 1 minute.

7. Pour broth mixture, stirring continuously for about 1 minute.

8. Add coconut milk, coconut aminos, salt and black pepper and cook for about 10 minutes, stirring occasionally.

9. Stir in zucchini and cook for about 2 minutes.

10. Transfer the zucchini mixture into a serving plate and top with steak slices.

11. Garnish with parsley and serve.

Ginger Carrot with Grouper Fillets

Time: 25 minutes

Servings: 4

Ingredients:

For Grouper:

2 tablespoons olive oil

1 tablespoon minced garlic

1 tablespoon minced ginger

Salt and freshly ground black pepper, to taste

4 grouper fillets

For Carrot:

2 tablespoons oil

4 large carrots, peeled and spiralized with Blade C

½ teaspoon red pepper flakes, crushed

Salt and Freshly Ground Black Pepper, to taste

Directions:

1. For grouper fillets in a large bowl, mix together all ingredients.
2. Refrigerate for about 2-3 hours.
3. Preheat the grill to high heat.
4. Grease the grill grate.
5. Place the grouper fillets on the hot grill with the flesh side down and cook for about 3-4 minutes per side.
6. Meanwhile in a skillet, heat oil on medium heat.
7. Add carrot and seasoning and cook for about 4-5 minutes.
8. Divide the carrot noodles in serving plates and top with fish fillets.

Cod Fillets Spinach Zucchini

Time: 25 minutes

Servings: 2

Ingredients:

For Cod:

1 (8-ounce) black cod fillet

Salt and freshly ground black pepper, to taste

For Spinach & Zucchini:

1 tablespoon sunflower oil

1 teaspoon fresh ginger, minced

1 garlic clove, minced

2 cups fresh spinach, torn

¾ cup vegetable broth

1 tablespoon soy sauce

Salt and freshly ground black pepper, to taste

2 medium zucchinis, spiralized with Blade C

¼ cup scallions, chopped

Directions:

1. Preheat the grill to medium-high heat.
2. Grease the grill grate.
3. Season the cod fillet with salt and black pepper.
4. Grill for about 4-5 minutes per side.
5. Slice the cod in 2 pieces and keep aside.
6. Meanwhile in a large skillet, heat oil on medium heat.
7. Add ginger and garlic and sauté for about 1 minute.
8. Add spinach and cook for about 1 minute.
9. Add broth, soy sauce, salt and black pepper and cook for about 1-2 minutes.
10. Stir in zucchini and cook for about 3-4 minutes.
11. Transfer the zucchini mixture into 2 serving plates and top with cod pieces.
12. Garnish with scallion and serve.

Delicious Zucchini, Chard & Cod Parcel

Time: 35 minutes

Servings: 2

Ingredients:

12-ounce wild cod

1 tomato, chopped

2 zucchini, spiralized with Blade C

4 scallions, chopped

6-8 baby chard leaves

1 tablespoon fresh lime juice

2 tablespoons fresh parsley leaves, chopped

¼-ounce chilled butter, chopped

1/8 teaspoon smoked paprika

Salt and freshly ground black pepper, to taste

Directions:

1. Preheat the oven to 350 degrees F.

2. Arrange a large parchment paper onto a smooth surface.

3. Place the cod in the center of parchment paper.

4. Top the cod with remaining ingredients and fold into a pouch to seal the filling.

5. Bake for about 20 minutes.

Garlic Ground Beef & Zucchini

Time: 30 minutes

Servings: 4

Ingredients:

1 tablespoon olive oil

1 medium onion, chopped

2 garlic cloves, minced

1 pound lean ground beef

¼ cup beef broth

1 cup cherry tomatoes, halved

3 medium zucchinis, spiralized with Blade C

Salt and freshly ground black pepper, to taste

3 tablespoons fresh basil, chopped

Directions:

1. In a large skillet heat oil on medium heat.

2. Add garlic and sauté for about 1 minute.

3. Add beef and cook for about 4-5 minutes.

4. Add broth, tomatoes and cook for about 4-5 minutes.

5. Stir in zucchini, salt and black pepper and cook for about 3-4 minutes.

6. Stir in basil and remove from heat.

7. Serve hot.

Avocado Zucchini Ground Beef

Time: 45 minutes

Servings: 2

Ingredients:

1 tablespoon olive oil

¼ cup white onion, chopped

1 garlic clove, minced

½ pound lean ground beef

1 teaspoon dried thyme, crushed

Salt and freshly ground black pepper, to taste

¼ cup beef broth

2 large tomatoes, seeded and chopped

3 zucchinis, spiralized with Blade C

1 cup black olives, pitted and halved

1 large avocado, peeled, pitted and cubed

Directions:

1. In a large skillet, heat oil on medium heat.

2. Add onion and sauté for 4-5 minutes.

3. Add garlic and sauté for about 1 minute.

4. Add beef and sprinkle with thyme, salt and black pepper and cook for about 10 minutes, stirring occasionally.

5. Add broth and cook for about 3-4 minutes.

6. Add tomatoes and cook for about 1-2 minutes, stirring occasionally.

7. Stir in remaining ingredients and cook for about 2-3 minutes.

8. Serve hot.

Ground Beef Mushrooms Basil & Zucchini

Time: 25 minutes

Servings: 4

Ingredients:

For Beef Mixture:

1 tablespoon olive oil

1 large onion, chopped

2 carrots, peeled and chopped

2 cups baby Bella mushrooms, chopped

2 garlic cloves, crushed

1 pound ground beef

2 tomatoes, chopped

1 (6-ounce) can tomato paste

1/3 cup red wine

1 tablespoon Italian seasoning

1 tablespoon fresh basil

1 teaspoon garlic powder

Salt and freshly ground black pepper, to taste

For Zucchini:

2 tablespoons olive oil

4 medium zucchinis, spiralized with Blade C

Salt and freshly ground black pepper, to taste

Directions:

1. In a large skillet, heat oil on medium heat.

2. Add onion, carrots and mushrooms and garlic and cook for about 3-5 minutes.

3. Add beef and cook for about 4-5 minutes.

4. Add tomatoes, tomato paste and cook for about 1-2 minutes.

5. Add red wine, Italian seasoning, salt, pepper, ground garlic and red pepper flakes and bring to a boil.

6. Reduce the heat and simmer for about 15 minutes or till desired thickness.

7. Meanwhile in a large skillet, heat oil on medium heat.

8. Add zucchini, salt and black pepper and cook for about 3-4 minutes.

9. Divide zucchini noodles in serving plates and top with beef mixture.

10. Serve hot.

Rosemary Ground Beef Zucchini

Time: 45 minutes

Servings: 2

Ingredients:

1 tablespoon olive oil

1/3 cup onion, chopped

2 garlic cloves, minced

1 teaspoon dried rosemary, crushed

1/8 teaspoon red pepper flakes, crushed

½ pound lean ground beef

2 medium tomatoes, chopped finely

Salt and freshly ground black pepper, to taste

¼ cup beef broth

2 medium zucchinis, spiralized with Blade C

½ cup canned red kidney beans, rinsed and drained

½ cup black olives, pitted and sliced

2 tablespoons fresh parsley leaves, chopped

Directions:

1. In a large skillet, heat oil on medium heat.
2. Add onion and sauté for about 4-5 minutes.
3. Add garlic, rosemary and red pepper flakes and sauté for about 1 minute.
4. Add beef and cook for about 5-7 minutes.
5. Add tomatoes, salt and black pepper and cook for about 3-4 minutes.
6. Add broth and bring to a boil.
7. Cook for about 2-3 minutes.
8. Add zucchini, beans and olives and cook for about 3-4 minutes.
9. Garnish with parsley and serve.

Mushrooms Onion Haddock Fillets Zucchini

Time: 45 minutes

Servings: 4

Ingredients:

2 tablespoons olive oil

1 medium white onion, sliced

½ teaspoon dried rosemary, crushed

2 cups portabella mushrooms, sliced

Salt and freshly ground black pepper, to taste

2 large zucchinis, spiralized with Blade C

4 (4-ounce) haddock fillets

Directions:

1. *Preheat the oven to 450 degrees F.*
2. *Grease a baking dish.*
3. *In a large skillet, heat oil on medium heat.*
4. *Add onion and sauté for about 2-3 minutes.*
5. *Add rosemary and mushrooms and sauté for about 3-4 minute.*
6. *Add zucchini, salt and black pepper and sauté for about 3 minutes.*
7. *Sprinkle fish fillets with salt and black pepper from both sides.*
8. *Arrange fish fillets in prepared baking dish in a single layer.*
9. *Top with zucchini mixture.*
10. *Cover the baking dish with a piece of foil and bake for about 15-20 minutes or till desired doneness.*

Butternut Squash with Broccoli & Herring

Time: 40 minutes

Servings: 4

Ingredients:

For Herring:

2 tablespoons olive oil

¼ cup tamari

1 tablespoon fresh lime juice

2 teaspoons white sesame seeds

Salt and freshly ground black pepper, to taste

4 (3-ounce) herring fillets

For Vegetables:

2 large butternut squash, peeled and spiralized with Blade C

2 cups broccoli florets

3 tablespoons extra virgin olive oil

2 teaspoons fresh ginger, minced

2 teaspoons garlic, minced

3 tablespoons honey

¼ cup tamari

2 teaspoons white sesame seeds

Salt and freshly ground black pepper, to taste

1 teaspoon black sesame seeds

Directions:

1. Preheat the oven to 400 degrees F.
2. Lightly, grease a baking dish.
3. For fish in a large bowl, add all ingredients and toss to coat well.
4. Refrigerate to marinade for at least 10 minutes.
5. Arrange fish fillets in prepared baking dish in a single layer.
6. Bake for about 10 minutes.
7. Remove baking dish from oven.
8. Place the squash noodles in baking dish and bake for about 6-7 minutes.
9. Meanwhile in a pan of boiling water, add broccoli and cook for about 3-4 minutes.
10. Drain well and keep aside.
11. In a large skillet, heat oil on medium heat.
12. Add ginger and garlic and sauté for about 1 minute.
13. Stir in broccoli noodles and remaining ingredients except black sesame seeds.
14. Transfer the squash noodles in skillet and cook for about 1-2 minutes.
15. In a serving dish, place squash mixture and top with fish fillets.
16. Garnish with black sesame seeds and serve.

Lemon Garlic Zucchini with Salmon

Time: 35 minutes

Servings: 4

Ingredients:

For Salmon:

1 tablespoon fresh ginger, minced

3 garlic cloves, minced

1 tablespoon fresh thyme, minced

2 tablespoons olive oil

2 tablespoons fresh lemon juice

Salt and freshly ground black pepper, to taste

4 (4-ounce) salmon fillets

For Zucchini:

1 tablespoon olive oil

2 garlic cloves, minced

4 medium zucchinis, spiralized with Blade C

Salt and freshly ground black pepper, to taste

2 tablespoons fresh lemon juice

¼ cup fresh parsley leaves, chopped

Directions:

1. For salmon in a large bowl, add all ingredients and mix well.
2. Refrigerate for at least 1-2 hours.
3. Preheat the grill to medium heat.
4. Grease the grill grate.
5. Grill the salmon for about 6-8 minutes per side.
6. Remove from grill and keep aside.
7. Meanwhile for zucchini in another large skillet, heat oil on medium heat.
8. Add garlic and sauté for about 1 minute.
9. Add zucchini, salt and black pepper and cook for about 2-3 minutes.
10. Stir in lemon juice and parsley and remove from heat.
11. Divide the zucchini mixture into serving plates and top with salmon fillets.
12. Serve hot.

Yummy Yellow Squash Curry with Beef & Zucchini

Time: 40 minutes

Servings: 4

Ingredients:

2 tablespoons olive oil, divided

1 pound boneless beef, trimmed and cut into thin strips

Salt and freshly ground black pepper, to taste

1 medium white onion, chopped

1 red bell pepper, seeded and chopped

1 garlic clove, minced

1 teaspoon fresh ginger, minced

1 teaspoon curry powder

1 cup coconut milk

2 medium zucchini, spiralized with Blade C

2 medium yellow squash, spiralized with Blade C

2 tablespoons fresh lime juice

2 tablespoon fresh cilantro leaves, chopped

1 teaspoon lime zest, grated freshly

Directions:

1. In a large pan, heat 1 tablespoon of oil on medium heat.

2. Add beef and sprinkle with salt and black pepper and cook for about 4-5 minutes or till browned.

3. Transfer the beef into a bowl.

4. In the same pan, heat remaining oil on medium heat.

5. Add onion and bell pepper and sauté for about 3-4 minutes.

6. Add garlic and curry powder and sauté for about 1 minute.

7. Slowly, add coconut milk and bring to a boil.

8. Stir in beef and cook for about 4-5 minutes.

9. Add zucchini and squash and cook for about 4-5 minutes.

10. Stir in lime juice, salt and black pepper and remove from heat.

11. Garnish with cilantro and lime zest and serve hot.

Curry Kale Steak & Yellow Squash

Time: 35 minutes

Servings: 2

Ingredients:

For Beef

¼ cup soy sauce

1 tablespoon fresh lime juice

1 tablespoon olive oil

Salt and freshly ground black pepper, to taste

½ pound sirloin steak, trimmed and sliced thinly

For Yellow Squash:

1 tablespoon olive oil

½ small onion, chopped

1 celery rib, chopped

1 garlic clove, minced

1 teaspoon fresh ginger, minced

1 jalapeño pepper, chopped

¼ cup soy sauce

Salt and freshly ground black pepper, to taste

2 medium yellow squash, spiralized with Blade C

1 cup fresh kale, trimmed and chopped

Salt and freshly ground black pepper, to taste

1 tablespoon black sesame seeds

Directions:

1. For steak in a large bowl, mix together all ingredients except steak.
2. Add steak slices and coat with marinade generously.
3. Refrigerate, covered for at least 2-3 hours.
4. Heat a large nonstick skillet on medium heat.
5. Add beef with marinade and cook for about 5-6 minutes.
6. Remove from heat and keep aside.
7. In another large skillet, heat oil on medium heat.
8. Add onion and celery and sauté for about 3-4 minutes.
9. Add garlic, ginger and jalapeño pepper and sauté for about 1 minute.
10. Add soy sauce and cook for about 1-2 minutes.
11. Stir in squash noodles, salt and black pepper and cook for about 3-4 minutes.
12. Divide squash noodles in serving plates and top with beef.
13. Garnish with sesame seeds and serve.

Salmon Zucchini with Spinach

Time: 35 minutes

Servings: 2

Ingredients:

For Salmon:

2 (4-ounce) salmon fillets

2 tablespoons extra virgin olive oil

1 tablespoon fresh lime juice

½ teaspoon garlic powder

Salt and freshly ground black pepper, to taste

For Vegetables:

1 tablespoon olive oil

2 teaspoons fresh ginger, minced

2 garlic cloves, minced

2 cups fresh spinach, torn

1½ cups vegetable broth

3 zucchinis, spiralized with Blade C

½ cup scallions, chopped

Salt and freshly ground black pepper, to taste

Directions:

1. Preheat the grill to medium heat.
2. Grease the grill grate.
3. Drizzle the salmon fillets with oil and lime juice and sprinkle with seasoning.
4. Grill the salmon fillets for about 6-8 minutes per side.
5. Meanwhile in a skillet, heat oil on medium heat.
6. Add ginger and garlic and sauté for about 1 minute.
7. Add spinach and cook for about 1-2 minutes.
8. Add broth and cook for 2-3 minutes.
9. Stir in zucchini noodles and cook for about 3-5 minutes.
10. Stir in scallion and remove from heat.
11. In a serving plate place zucchini mixture. Top with salmon and serve.

Soy Sauce Zucchini with Mushrooms & Salmon

Time: 35 minutes

Servings: 2

Ingredients:

For Salmon:

1 (8-ounce) salmon fillet, cubed

1 tablespoon olive oil

2 tablespoons soy sauce

Salt and freshly ground black pepper, to taste

For Vegetables:

1 tablespoon olive oil

1 teaspoon garlic, minced

¼ teaspoon fresh ginger, minced

1 cup shiitake mushrooms, stemmed and sliced

3 medium zucchinis, spiralized with Blade C

Salt and freshly ground black pepper, to taste

Directions:

1. Preheat the oven to 400 degrees F.

2. Lightly, grease a baking dish.

3. In a bowl, add salmon and all ingredients and toss to coat well.

4. Transfer the salmon in prepared baking dish.

5. Bake for about 15 minutes.
6. Remove from oven and cut the salmon into small pieces.
7. Meanwhile in a large skillet, heat oil on medium heat.
8. Add garlic and ginger and sauté for about 1 minute.
9. Add mushrooms and cook for about 5 minutes.
10. Add zucchini, salt and black pepper and cook for about 3-4 minutes.
11. Stir in salmon and remove from heat.
12. Serve hot.

Delicious Salmon Casserole & Zucchini

Time: 1 hour 25 minutes

Servings: 4

Ingredients:

3 tablespoons olive oil, divided

1 small onion, chopped

1 celery stalk, chopped

3 garlic cloves, minced

Salt and freshly ground black pepper, to taste

2 medium zucchinis, Spiralized with Blade C

1¼ cups cooked salmon, chopped very finely

1 tablespoon arrowroot powder

1½ cups unsweetened almond milk

Directions:

1. Preheat the oven to 350 degrees F.
2. Lightly, grease a casserole dish.
3. In a skillet, heat 1 tablespoon of oil on medium heat.
4. Add onion and celery and sauté for about 3-4 minutes.
5. Add garlic and sauté for about 1 minute.
6. Stir in zucchini, salmon, salt and black pepper.
7. Transfer the zucchini mixture in a casserole dish.
8. In another pan, heat oil on medium-low heat.
9. Add arrowroot powder, beating continuously for about 1 minute.
10. Slowly, add almond milk, beating continuously and cook for about 2-3 minutes or till thick.
11. Pour sauce over zucchini mixture evenly.
12. Bake for about 45-60 minutes.

Yellow Squash with Beef Meatballs

Time: 60 minutes

Servings: 4

Ingredients:

For Meatballs:

1 pound lean ground beef

2 tablespoons chia seeds

2 garlic cloves, minced

2 tablespoons tomato puree

1 tablespoon fresh thyme, minced

Salt and freshly ground black pepper, to taste

2 teaspoons olive oil

For Squash:

½ tablespoon olive oil

1 medium onion, chopped

1 garlic clove, minced

2 tablespoons fresh thyme, chopped

½ cup beef broth

2 tablespoons fresh lemon juice

1½ cups fresh tomatoes, chopped finely

1½ cups tomato puree

Salt and freshly ground black pepper, to taste

3 large yellow squash, spiralized with Blade C

Directions:

1. For meatballs in a large bowl, mix together all ingredients except oil.
2. Keep aside for at least 10 minutes.
3. Make desired sized balls from mixture.
4. In a large skillet, heat oil on medium heat.
5. Add meatballs and cook for about 3-4 minutes.
6. Transfer into a plate and keep aside.
7. For Sauce in the same skillet, heat oil on medium heat.
8. Add onion and sauté for about 4-5 minutes.

9. Add garlic and thyme and sauté for about 1 minute.

10. Add broth and lemon juice and cook for about 1 minute.

11. Add remaining ingredients except squash noodles and cook for about 10-15 minutes.

12. Stir in meatballs and immediately, reduce the heat to medium-low.

13. Simmer for about 10-15 minutes.

14. Add squash noodles and cook for about 2-3 minutes.

15. Serve immediately.

Asparagus Sirloin Steak & Sweet Potato

Time: 50 minutes

Servings: 2

Ingredients:

2 tablespoons olive oil

¾ pound sirloin steak, trimmed and cut into thin strips

Salt and freshly ground black pepper, to taste

¼ cup onion, chopped

1 garlic clove, minced

10 asparagus spears, trimmed and cut into 1-inch pieces

1 small red bell pepper, seeded and sliced thinly

1½ cups fresh tomatoes, chopped finely

¼ cup beef broth

1 large sweet potato, peeled and spiralized with Blade C

1 tablespoon fresh parsley leaves, chopped

Directions:

1. In a large skillet, heat 1 tablespoon of oil on medium heat.
2. Add beef and sprinkle with salt and black pepper and cook for about 3-4 minutes or till browned from all sides.
3. Transfer the beef into a bowl.
4. In the same skillet, heat remaining oil on medium heat.
5. Add onion and sauté for about 3-4 minutes.
6. Add garlic and sauté for about 1 minute.
7. Add asparagus and bell pepper and cook for about 8-10 minutes.
8. Add tomatoes, salt and black pepper and cook for about 2 minutes, mashing with the back of spoon.
9. Add broth and cook for about 2 minutes.
10. Stir in sweet potato and cook for about 5 minutes.
11. Stir in beef and cook for about 2-3 minutes.
12. Garnish with parsley and serve.

Veggies Mixed Beef & Sweet Potato

Time: 60 minutes

Servings: 4

Ingredients:

1½ tablespoons extra virgin coconut oil

1 large onion, chopped

1 cup celery, chopped

2 carrots, peeled and chopped

1 cup green bell pepper, seeded and chopped

1 pound beef stew meat, trimmed and cubed

3-4 fresh tomatoes, chopped finely

1½ cups tomato puree

½ cup beef broth

1 tablespoon dried basil, crushed

Salt and freshly ground black pepper, to taste

2 large sweet potatoes, peeled and spiralized with Blade C

2 tablespoons fresh scallions, chopped

Directions:

1. In a large skillet, heat oil on medium heat.

2. Add onion, celery, carrots and bell peppers and sauté for about 4-5 minutes.

3. Add beef and cook for about 10 minutes, stirring occasionally.

4. Add tomatoes and cook for 1-2 minutes, crushing them.
5. Add remaining ingredients except sweet potato and bring to a boil.
6. Reduce the heat to low and simmer, covered for about 10-15 minutes.
7. Stir in sweet potato noodles and cook for about 8-10 minutes.
8. Garnish with scallion and serve.

Coconut Turnip & Salmon Curry

Time: 25 minutes

Servings: 4

Ingredients:

1 tablespoon coconut oil

2 garlic cloves, minced

2 teaspoons fresh ginger, minced

3 scallions, chopped (white and green parts separated)

3 teaspoons Thai red curry paste

1 (13½-ounce) can coconut milk (chilled)

1¼ cups vegetable broth

2 medium turnips, trimmed, peeled and spiralized with Blade D

5-ounce fresh green beans, trimmed and cut into ½-inch pieces

6-ounce skinless salmon fillet, cut into chunks

¼ cup fresh basil leaves, chopped

Directions:

1. In a large skillet, heat oil on medium-high heat.
2. Add garlic, ginger, and white part of the scallions and sauté for about 1 minute.
3. Add curry paste and sauté for about 1 minute.
4. Carefully, scoop the coconut cream from the top of the can of coconut milk.
5. Add the coconut cream into the skillet and stir to combine.
6. Cook for about 1 minute, stirring continuously.
7. Add the remaining coconut milk and broth and bring to a boil.
8. Stir in the turnip noodles, green beans and salmon chunks.
9. Reduce heat to low and simmer, covered for about 5-7 minutes or till desired doneness.
10. Serve hot with the garnishing of basil.

Sardines Zucchini

Time: 30 minutes

Servings: 4

Ingredients:

For Sardines:

4 medium whole fresh sardines, gutted, rinsed and patted dry

1½ tablespoons olive oil

2 tablespoons fresh lemon juice

Salt and freshly ground black pepper, to taste

For Zucchini:

1 tablespoon olive oil

1 garlic clove, minced

1 jalapeño pepper, seeded and chopped

3 large zucchinis, spiralized with Blade C

Salt and freshly ground black pepper, to taste

1 tablespoon fresh lemon juice

1 teaspoon lemon zest, grated freshly

Directions:

1. Preheat the grill to medium-high heat.
2. Grease the grill grate.
3. In a large baking dish, place sardines.
4. Drizzle with oil and lemon juice and sprinkle with salt and black pepper.
5. Grill for about 5 minutes, flipping once in the middle way.
6. Transfer the sardines into a large dish and cover with a piece of foil to keep warm.
7. For zucchini in a large skillet, heat oil on medium heat.
8. Add garlic and jalapeño pepper and sauté for about 1 minute.
9. Add zucchini, salt and black pepper and cook for about 3-4 minutes.
10. Stir in lemon juice and remove from heat.
11. Transfer the zucchini mixture into serving plates evenly.
12. Place sardines alongside the zucchini evenly.
13. Garnish with lemon zest and serve.

Rosemary Tuna Asparagus Zucchini

Time: 25 minutes

Servings: 2

Ingredients:

For Tuna:

1 small garlic clove, minced

1 teaspoon fresh ginger, minced

1 teaspoon dried rosemary, crushed

1 tablespoon olive oil

1 tablespoon soy sauce

½ tablespoon fresh lime juice

2 (1-inch thick) tuna steaks

For Zucchini & Asparagus:

4 garlic cloves, minced and divided

3 cups fresh basil leaves, chopped

½ cup plus 1 tablespoon olive oil

½ cup walnuts, chopped

Salt and freshly ground black pepper, to taste

½ pound asparagus, trimmed and cut into 1½-inch pieces

3 medium zucchinis, spiralized with Blade C

Directions:

1. For tuna in a large bowl, add all ingredients and toss to coat well.

2. Refrigerate, covered for at least 1 hour.

3. Preheat the broiler of oven.

4. Arrange the rack 4-inch from heating element.

5. Broil the tuna steaks for about 3 minutes per side.

6. In a food processor, add 3 garlic cloves, basil, ½ cup of oil, walnuts, salt and black pepper and pulse till smooth. Keep aside.

7. In a skillet, heat remaining oil on medium heat.

8. Add remaining garlic and sauté for about 1 minute.

9. Add asparagus and cook for about 4-5 minutes.

10. Meanwhile in a pan of boiling water, add zucchini noodles and cook for about 2-3 minutes.

11. Drain well and pat dry with paper towel.

12. In a serving plate mix together zucchini, asparagus and basil mixture.

13. Top with tuna and serve.

Sweet Potato with Ground Beef

Time: 45 minutes

Servings: 4

Ingredients:

2 large sweet potatoes, peeled and spiralized with Blade C

1 tablespoon olive oil

1 white onion, chopped

2 garlic cloves, minced

1 pound lean ground beef

¼ teaspoon red chili powder

Salt and freshly ground black pepper, to taste

½ cup beef broth

3 cups fresh tomatoes, crushed

2 red bell peppers, seeded and chopped

1 tablespoon mixed dried herbs (thyme, oregano, marjoram, basil), crushed

¼ cup fresh cilantro leaves, chopped

Directions:

1. In a large pan of boiling water, add sweet potato noodles and cook for about 4-5 minutes.

2. Drain well and keep aside.

3. In a large skillet, heat oil on medium heat.

4. Add onion and sauté for about 8-9 minutes.

5. Add garlic and sauté for about 1 minute.

6. Add beef and sprinkle with chili powder, salt and black pepper and cook for about 10 minutes, stirring occasionally.

7. Add broth, tomatoes, bell pepper and herbs and cook for about 5-10 minutes, stirring occasionally.

8. In a serving plate place sweet potato and top with beef mixture.

9. Garnish with cilantro and serve.

Ginger Sweet Potato with Beef Meatballs

Time: 55 minutes

Servings: 4

Ingredients:

For Meatballs:

2 tablespoons olive oil, divided

1 small white onion, chopped finely

1 teaspoon fresh ginger, minced

2 garlic cloves, minced

1 pound lean ground beef

1 tablespoon fresh basil, chopped

Salt and freshly ground black pepper, to taste

½ cup fresh orange juice

¼ cup soy sauce

For Sweet Potato:

1½ tablespoons olive oil

2 garlic cloves, minced

½ teaspoon red pepper flakes, crushed

2 large sweet potatoes, peeled and spiralized with Blade C

Salt and freshly ground black pepper, to taste

Directions:

1. For meatballs in a large skillet heat 1 tablespoon of oil on medium heat.

2. Add onion and sauté for about 7-8 minutes.

3. Add ginger and garlic and sauté for about 1 minute.

4. Transfer the onion mixture into a bowl and keep aside to cool completely.

5. Add beef, basil, salt and black pepper in bowl with onion mixture and mix till well combined.

6. Make small sized balls from mixture.

7. In the same skillet, heat remaining oil on medium heat.

8. Add meatballs and cook for about 2-3 minutes per side or till browned.

9. Add orange juice and soy sauce and cook, covered for about 8-10 minutes.

10. Transfer the balls into a bowl.

11. Increase the heat to medium-high and cook for about 5-10 minutes or till desired thickness.

12. Remove from heat and stir in meatballs.

13. For sweet potato in another large skillet, heat oil on medium heat.

14. Add garlic and red pepper flakes and sauté for about 1 minute.

15. Add sweet potato, salt and black pepper and cook for about 6-8 minutes.

16. Transfer the sweet potato mixture in large serving bowls.

17. Top with meatball sauce and serve.

Chili Zucchini with Tomatoes & Shrimp

Time: 25 minutes

Servings: 2

Ingredients:

1 tablespoon coconut oil, divided

3 garlic cloves, minced and divided

½ pound shrimp, peeled and deveined

2 large zucchinis, spiralized with Blade C

1/8 teaspoon chili powder

Salt and freshly ground black pepper, to taste

½ cup cherry tomatoes, halved

1 tablespoon fresh lime juice

Directions:

1. In a large skillet, heat ½ tablespoon of oil on medium-high heat.
2. Add 2 garlic cloves and sauté for about 30 seconds.
3. Add shrimp and sprinkle with seasoning and cook for about 3-4 minutes.
4. Transfer the shrimp into a plate and keep aside.
5. In the same skillet, heat remaining oil on medium heat.
6. Add remaining garlic and sauté for about 30 seconds.
7. Add zucchini and cook for 1-2 minutes.
8. Stir in tomatoes, shrimp and lime juice and cook for about 1 minute.
9. Remove from heat and serve immediately.

Honey Broccoli Zucchini Shrimp

Time: 30 minutes

Servings: 2

Ingredients:

3 tablespoons soy sauce

1 teaspoon balsamic vinegar

1 teaspoon honey

1½ tablespoons olive oil

¼ cup onion, chopped

2 garlic cloves, minced

½ teaspoon fresh ginger, minced

1 cup broccoli florets

4 jumbo shrimp, peeled and deveined

1 large zucchini, spiralized with Blade C

Salt and freshly ground black pepper, to taste

¼ teaspoon black sesame seeds

Directions:

1. In a bowl, mix together soy sauce, vinegar and honey. Keep aside.

2. In a large skillet, heat oil on medium heat.

3. Add onion and sauté for about 4-5 minutes.

4. Add garlic and ginger and sauté for about 1 minute.

5. Add broccoli and cook for about 3-4 minutes. Add shrimp and cook for about 2 minutes.

6. Flip the side of shrimp and stir in zucchini, salt, black pepper and soy sauce mixture and cook for about 2-3 minutes. Garnish with sesame seeds and serve.

Parsley Zucchini with Asparagus & Shrimp

Time: 25 minutes

Servings: 4

Ingredients:

2 tablespoons olive oil

2 garlic cloves, minced

1 cup asparagus, trimmed and cut into 1-inch pieces

4 medium zucchinis, spiralized with Blade C

1 teaspoon soy sauce

1 pound shrimp, peeled and deveined

Salt and freshly ground black pepper, to taste

3 tablespoons fresh parsley, chopped

1 tablespoon black sesame seeds

Directions:

1. In a skillet, heat oil on medium heat.

2. Add garlic and sauté for about 1 minute.

3. Add asparagus and zucchini and cook for about 2-3 minutes.

4. Add soy sauce and shrimp and cook for about 4 minutes.

5. Stir in parsley and immediately remove from heat.

6. Garnish with sesame seeds and serve hot.

Delicious Sweet Potato & Beef Meatballs Curry

Time: 55 minutes

Servings: 4

Ingredients:

For Meatballs:

1 pound lean ground beef

1 tablespoon garlic, minced

1 tablespoon fresh ginger, minced

¼ cup yellow onion, chopped finely

1 cup brown mushrooms, chopped finely

1 jalapeño pepper, minced

1 teaspoon Sriracha

½ teaspoon fish sauce

Salt and freshly ground black pepper, to taste

1 large egg

1 tablespoon cornstarch

For Curry Sauce:

1 (13½-ounce) can coconut milk

2 tablespoons red curry paste

2 teaspoons honey

½ teaspoon fish sauce

For Sweet Potatoes:

1 tablespoon olive oil

2 large sweet potatoes, peeled and spiralized with Blade C

Salt and freshly ground black pepper, to taste

Directions:

1. Preheat the oven to 400 degrees F. Line a large baking sheet with a greased piece of foil.
2. In a large bowl, add all ingredients and mix till well combined.
3. Make small sized balls from the mixture.
4. Arrange the meatballs onto prepared baking sheet in a single layer.
5. Bake for about 13 minutes.
6. Flip and cook for about 2-3 minutes.
7. Remove from oven and keep aside.
8. For curry sauce in a large pan, add coconut milk on medium-high heat and bring to a boil.
9. Add the red curry paste and beat till well combined.
10. Stir in honey and fish sauce.
11. Carefully, add the meatballs and reduce the heat to medium-low.
12. Simmer for about 10 minutes.
13. Meanwhile in a large skillet, heat oil on medium-high heat.
14. Add sweet potatoes and cook for about 6-8 minutes.
15. Season with salt and pepper and remove from heat.
16. Divide sweet potato noodles into serving bowls and top with meatballs and curry sauce. Serve hot.

Thyme Cabbage with Ground Beef

Time: 45 minutes

Servings: 4

Ingredients:

1 tablespoon Extra Virgin Olive Oil

1 Yellow Onion, chopped

2 Large Red Bell Peppers, seeded and chopped

1 Pound Lean Ground Beef

1 teaspoon Dried thyme, crushed

1 Medium Head Cabbage, spiralized with Blade C

3 cups Fresh Roma Tomatoes, pureed

Salt and freshly ground black pepper, to taste

1/3 cup Fresh Parsley, chopped

Directions:

1. In a large skillet, heat oil on medium heat.

2. Add onion and bell peppers and sauté for about 4-5 minutes.

3. Add beef and thyme and cook for about 8-10 minutes.

4. Stir in cabbage noodles, tomato puree and seasoning.

5. Reduce the heat to low and simmer for about 10-15 minutes.

6. Garnish with parsley and serve.

Sweet & Sour Balsamic Cabbage Ground Beef

Time: 30 minutes

Servings: 4

Ingredients:

1 teaspoon olive oil

1 pound lean ground beef

1 medium head cabbage, spiralized with Blade C

1/3 cup almond butter

1 tablespoon coconut oil, melted

3 tablespoons tamari

2 tablespoons balsamic vinegar

1 tablespoon honey

1 tablespoon sesame seeds, toasted

Directions:

1. In a large nonstick skillet, heat oil on medium-high heat.

2. Add beef and cook for about 4-5 minutes.

3. Spread cabbage noodles over beef evenly and cook, covered for about 10 minutes.

4. Uncover and cook for about 5 minutes more.

5. In a small bowl, add remaining ingredients except sesame seeds and beat till well combined.

6. Pour butter mixture over cabbage noodles and cook for about 2 minutes or till heated completely.

7. Garnish with sesame seeds and serve.

Garlic Carrot with Steak

Time: 30 minutes

Servings: 2

Ingredients:

2 tablespoon olive oil, divided

8-ounce sirloin steak, trimmed and cut into thin strips

½ teaspoon cayenne pepper

Salt and freshly ground black pepper, to taste

1 garlic clove, minced

1 Serrano pepper, seeded and minced

2 cups carrot, peeled and spiralized with Blade C

¼ cup Parmesan cheese, shredded

Directions:

1. In a large skillet, heat 1 tablespoon of oil on medium heat.

2. Add beef and sprinkle with cayenne pepper, salt and black pepper and sear for about 5 minutes or till browned from all sides.

3. Transfer the beef into a large bowl.

4. In the same skillet, heat remaining oil on medium heat.

5. Add garlic and Serrano pepper and sauté for about 30 seconds.

6. Add carrot noodles and cook for about 3-4 minutes.

7. Stir in steak slices, salt and black pepper and cook for about 1-2 minutes.

8. Serve hot with the sprinkling of cheese.

Soy Sauce Zucchini Prawns

Time: 30 minutes

Servings: 2

Ingredients:

3 garlic cloves, minced and divided

¼ teaspoon fresh ginger, minced

1 teaspoon soy sauce

1 teaspoon honey

½ teaspoon red pepper flakes, crushed

12 fresh king prawns, peeled and deveined

3 tablespoons coconut oil, divided

2 large zucchinis, spiralized with Blade C

Salt and freshly ground black pepper, to taste

1 tablespoon fresh lemon juice

2 tablespoons fresh parsley, chopped

Directions:

1. In a large bowl, mix together 2 garlic cloves, ginger, soy sauce, honey and ¼ teaspoon of red pepper flakes.

2. Add prawns and coat with marinade generously.

3. Refrigerate, covered to marinate for at least 2-3 hours.

4. In a large skillet, heat 2 tablespoons of oil on medium heat.

5. Add prawns with marinade and stir fry for about 2-4 minutes.

6. Remove from heat and keep warm.

7. In another large skillet, heat remaining oil on medium heat.

8. Add remaining garlic and sauté for about 1 minute.

9. Add zucchini, remaining red pepper flakes, salt and black pepper and cook for about 2-3 minutes.

10. Stir in lemon juice and remove from the heat.

11. Transfer the zucchini mixture into a serving plate and top with prawns.

12. Garnish with parsley and serve hot.

Chili Sweet Potato with Calms

Time: 30 minutes

Servings: 2

Ingredients:

1 tablespoon olive oil

1 small white onion, chopped

1 celery stalk, chopped

2 small garlic cloves, minced

¼ cup fish broth

1 tablespoon fresh lime juice

10 little neck clams

3 teaspoons fresh thyme, chopped

¼ teaspoon chili powder

Salt and freshly ground black pepper, to taste

1 large sweet potato, peeled and spiralized with Blade C

Directions:

1. In a skillet, heat oil on medium heat.
2. Add onion and celery and sauté for about 3-4 minutes.
3. Add garlic and sauté for about 1 minute.
4. Add broth and lime juice and bring to a boil.
5. Stir in clams and reduce the heat to medium-low.
6. Simmer, covered for about 6-7 minutes.
7. Stir in thyme and seasoning and immediately, remove from heat.
8. Meanwhile, place sweet potato noodles in a steamer basket.
9. Arrange the basket over a pan of boiling water and steam for about 6-8 minutes.
10. Transfer the sweet potato into a serving bowl.
11. Top with clam mixture and serve.

Hoisin Sauce Broccoli Steak

Time: 35 minutes

Servings: 2

Ingredients:

For Steak:

¼ cup hoisin sauce

¼ cup fresh orange juice

2 tablespoons soy sauce

1/8 teaspoon red pepper flakes, crushed

2 (5-ounce) (1-inch thick) sirloin steaks

1 tablespoon olive oil

For Broccoli:

2 cups broccoli florets

1 teaspoon olive oil

1 small white onion, chopped finely

1 tablespoon fresh ginger, minced

1 tablespoon garlic, minced

2 broccoli stems, spiralized with Blade C

Salt and freshly ground black pepper, to taste

Directions:

1. For steak in a bowl, mix together all ingredients except steaks and oil.

2. Add sirloin steaks and coat with marinade generously.

3. Refrigerate for at least 2 hours.

4. Remove the steak from refrigerator and keep in room temperature for about 5 minutes before cooking.

5. Remove the steaks from bowl, reserving the marinade for later.

6. In a nonstick skillet, heat olive oil on high heat.

7. Add steaks and cook for about 3 minutes per side.

8. Transfer the steaks onto a cutting board and cut into thin strips.

9. In the same skillet, add the reserved marinade on medium-low heat and bring to a gentle boil.

10. Simmer for about 2-3 minutes.

11. Meanwhile in a large pan of boiling water, cook the broccoli florets for about 3-4 minutes.
12. Drain well and immediately, place in ice water till chilled, and then drain well.
13. In a large nonstick skillet, heat oil on medium-high heat.
14. Add onions, ginger and garlic and sauté for about 1-2 minutes.
15. Add broccoli noodles, salt and black pepper and cook for about 3 minutes.
16. Add broccoli florets and cook for about 1-2 minutes.
17. Divide broccoli mixture into 2 serving plates and top with beef strops.
18. Pour marinade sauce on top and serve.

Cumin Celeriac with Ground Lamb

Time: 55 minutes

Servings: 4

Ingredients:

½ tablespoon olive oil

1 onion, chopped

1 garlic clove, minced

1 pound ground lamb

1 teaspoon ground cumin

1 tablespoon fresh rosemary, chopped

Salt and freshly ground black pepper, to taste

1 celeriac, peeled and spiralized with Blade C

½ cup celery rib, chopped

1 cup tomatoes, chopped finely

1 tablespoon tomato paste

¼ teaspoon red pepper flakes, crushed

½ cup low sodium chicken broth

Directions:

1. In a large skillet, heat oil on medium heat.

2. Add onion and garlic and sauté for about 2-3 minutes.

3. Add lamb and cook for about 8-10 minutes or till browned.

4. Add cumin, rosemary, salt and pepper and cook for about 1 minute.

5. Add Celeriac, celery rib, tomato, tomato paste and red pepper flakes and cook for about 2-3 minutes until vegetable are tender.

6. Add broth and bring to a boil on high heat.

7. Reduced heat to medium and cook, covered for about 10-15 minutes or till desired doneness.

Garlic Lamb Cutlets Sweet Potato

Time: 40 minutes

Servings: 4

Ingredients:

For Lamb Cutlets:

8 lamb cutlets, trimmed

½ tablespoon olive oil

2 tablespoons fresh rosemary, chopped

2 tablespoons fresh basil Leaves, chopped

Salt and freshly ground black pepper, to taste

For Sweet Potato:

2 tablespoons olive oil

1 garlic clove, minced

2 sweet potatoes, peeled and spiralized with Blade C

Salt and freshly ground black pepper, to taste

3 tablespoons fresh cilantro leaves, chopped

Directions:

1. *Preheat the oven to 425 degrees F.*
2. *Grease a baking dish.*
3. *Arrange lamb cutlets in prepared baking dish.*
4. *Drizzle with oil and sprinkle with herbs and seasoning generously.*

5. Bake for about 20 minutes, flipping once in the middle way.

6. Meanwhile in a large skillet, heat oil on medium heat.

7. Add garlic and sauté for about 1 minute.

8. Add sweet potato noodles, salt and black pepper and cook for about 8-10 minutes.

9. Divide the sweet potato noodles in serving plates and top with lamb cutlets.

10. Serve with the garnishing of cilantro.

Yummy Zucchini with Lamb Cutlets

Time: 30 minutes

Servings: 6

Ingredients:

For Lamb Cutlets:

2 garlic cloves, minced

2 tablespoons olive oil

2 teaspoons dried oregano, crushed

2 teaspoons sweet paprika

Salt and freshly ground black pepper, to taste

12 lamb cutlets, trimmed

For Zucchini:

3 tablespoons olive oil

6 large zucchinis, spiralized with Blade C

Salt and freshly ground black pepper, to taste

Directions:

1. Preheat the grill to high heat.
2. Grease the grill grate.
3. For lamb in a bowl mix together all ingredients except lamb cutlets.
4. Add cutlets and coat with garlic mixture evenly.
5. Keep aside for at least 10 minutes.
6. Grill the cutlets for about 2-3 minutes per side or till desired doneness.
7. Meanwhile in a large skillet, heat oil on medium heat.
8. Add zucchini, salt and black pepper and cook for about 3-4 minutes.
9. Divide the zucchini noodles in serving plates and top with lamb cutlets.
10. Serve immediately.

Garlic Scallops Zucchini

Time: 25 minutes

Servings: 4

Ingredients:

3 tablespoons olive oil, divided

2 garlic cloves, minced

6 medium zucchini, spiralized with Blade C

Salt and freshly ground black pepper, to taste

1 tablespoon fresh lemon juice

4 scallions, chopped (white and green part, separated)

1 pound bay scallops, cleaned, rinsed and pat dried

Directions:

1. In a large skillet, heat 2 tablespoons of oil on medium-high heat.

2. Add garlic and sauté for about 1 minute.

3. Add zucchini noodles, and sprinkle with salt and black pepper and cook for about 4-5 minutes.

4. Transfer the zucchini into a plate.

5. Add lime juice and white part of scallions and gently, stir t combine.

6. In the same skillet, heat remaining oil on medium-high heat.

7. Add scallops and cook for about 4 minutes, tossing once after 2 minutes.

8. Transfer the scallops into the plate with zucchini.

9. Top with green part of scallions and serve.

Scallops Zucchini with Spinach

Time: 20 minutes

Servings: 4

Ingredients:

For Scallops:

3 tablespoons bacon fat

3 garlic cloves, minced

1½ pounds large scallops

2 tablespoons fresh lemon juice

For Zucchini & Spinach:

3 tablespoons bacon fat

2 garlic cloves, minced

1 pound fresh spinach, chopped

3 large zucchinis, spiralized with Blade C

Directions:

1. For scallops in a large skillet, heat bacon fat on medium heat.
2. Add garlic and sauté for about 1 minute.
3. Add scallops and cook for about 1½ minutes per side.
4. Stir in lemon juice and cook for about 1 minute.
5. Transfer the scallops into a plate.
6. Meanwhile in another large skillet, heat bacon fat on medium heat.
7. Add garlic and sauté for about 1 minute.
8. Add zucchini noodles and spinach and cook for about 3-4 minutes.
9. Transfer the zucchini mixture into serving plate.
10. Place scallops over spinach with the sauce in pan and serve.

Delight Apple with Spinach & Scallops

Time: 25 minutes

Servings: 2

Ingredients:

2 tablespoon olive oil, divided

6 large scallops

1 green apple, peeled and spiralized with Blade C

1 cup fresh baby spinach

Salt and freshly ground black pepper, to taste

2 tablespoons freshly squeezed lemon juice

Directions:

1. In a large skillet, heat 2 tablespoon of oil on medium heat.

2. Add scallops and cook for 3-4 minutes.

3. Transfer the scallops into a plate.

4. In the same skillet, heat remaining oil on medium heat.

5. Add apple, spinach, salt and black pepper and cook for about 2-3 minutes.

6. Stir in lemon juice and remove from heat.

7. Transfer the apple mixture into serving plate.

8. Place scallops over spinach with the sauce in pan and serve.

Chili Zucchini Lobster

Time: 45 minutes

Servings: 2

Ingredients:

2 tablespoons coconut oil, divided

2 (4-ounce) lobster tails, shelled and cut into bite size pieces

½ small onion, chopped

2 garlic cloves, minced

2 cups fresh tomatoes, chopped finely

½ cup vegetable broth

¼ teaspoon chili powder

Salt and freshly ground black pepper, to taste

3 medium zucchinis, spiralized with Blade C

1 tablespoon fresh cilantro, chopped

Directions:

1. In a large skillet, heat 1 tablespoon of oil on medium heat.

2. Add lobster tails and cook for about 6-7 minutes.

3. Transfer the lobster into a serving plate.

4. In the same skillet, heat remaining oil on medium heat.

5. Add onion and sauté for 4-5 minutes.

6. Add garlic and sauté for about 1 minute.

7. Add tomatoes and cook for about 3-4 minutes, crushing them.

8. Add broth and seasoning and bring to a boil.

9. Reduce the heat to low and simmer for about 10-15 minutes.

10. Stir in zucchini and lobster meat and cook for about 5 minutes.

11. Garnish with cilantro and serve.

Lamb Meatballs With Zucchini

Time: 25 minutes

Servings: 4

Ingredients:

For Meatballs:

1 pound lean ground lamb

1 egg, beaten

2 garlic cloves, minced

1 medium white onion, chopped finely

¼ teaspoon ground cumin

Salt and freshly ground black pepper, to taste

1 tablespoon olive oil

For Zucchini:

1 tablespoon Extra Virgin Olive Oil

4 medium zucchinis, spiralized with Blade C

Salt and freshly ground black pepper, to taste

2 scallions, chopped

For Sauce:

1 cup fresh parsley leaves

1 cup fresh mint leaves

2 garlic cloves, minced

¼ cup extra-virgin olive oil

1 tablespoon fresh lime juice

Pinch of cayenne pepper

Salt and freshly ground black pepper, to taste

Directions:

1. Preheat the grill to high heat.

2. Grease the grill grate.

3. In a bowl, add all meatballs ingredients except oil and mix till well combined.

4. Make desired size balls from mixture.

5. Coat the balls with oil evenly.

6. Grill the balls for about 8 minutes, flipping once after 4 minutes.

7. Transfer the balls into a bowl.

8. Meanwhile for zucchini in a skillet, heat oil on medium heat.

9. Add zucchini, salt and black pepper and cook for about 3-4 minutes.

10. Transfer the zucchini into a large serving plate.

11. Meanwhile in a food processor, add all sauce ingredients and pulse till smooth.

12. Pour sauce over zucchini and gently, stir to combine.

13. Top with grilled meatballs and serve with the garnishing of cilantro.

Garlic Lamb Muffins With Zucchini

Time: 40 minutes

Servings: 4

Ingredients:

For Lamb Muffins:

1 pound lean ground lamb

¼ cup onion, chopped

1 garlic clove, minced

1 large egg, beaten

3 tablespoons almond flour

¼ teaspoon cayenne pepper

Salt and freshly ground black pepper, to taste

For Zucchini:

4 large zucchinis, spiralized with Blade C

Salt and freshly ground black pepper, to taste

2 cups fresh spinach

½ cup fresh basil, chopped

1 garlic clove, minced

½ cup walnuts, chopped

1 tablespoon fresh lime juice

¼-½ cup vegetable broth

Directions:

1. Preheat the oven to 375 degrees F.
2. Line a 12 cups muffin pan with paper liners.
3. In a large bowl, mix together all ingredients.
4. Make 12 even sized balls from mixture
5. Transfer the mixture into prepared muffin cups evenly.
6. Bake for about 20 minutes.
7. Meanwhile in a micro wave safe bowl, place ½ of the zucchini noodles and sprinkle with salt and black pepper.
8. Microwave on high for about 2 minutes.
9. Repeat with remaining zucchini noodles.
10. Transfer the zucchini in a large serving plate.
11. In a food processor, add remaining ingredients and pulse till smooth.
12. Pour spinach sauce over zucchini noodles and gently stir to combine.
13. Top with lamb muffins and serve.

Ginger Honey Turnip Tenderloin Pork

Time: 45 minutes

Servings: 2

Ingredients:

For Pork:

½ teaspoon fresh ginger, minced

2 garlic cloves, minced

1 tablespoon fresh rosemary, minced

2 tablespoons soy sauce

1 tablespoon fresh lemon juice

½ tablespoon honey

Salt and freshly ground black pepper, to taste

½ pound pork tenderloin, trimmed

For Turnip:

1 tablespoon olive oil

½ small white onion, chopped

2 garlic cloves, minced

1 Serrano pepper, seeded and minced

2 large turnips, trimmed, peeled and spiralized with Blade C

Salt and freshly ground black pepper, to taste

1 scallion, chopped

Directions:

1. In a large bowl, add all pork ingredients and toss to coat well.
2. Refrigerate for about 2-3 hours, tossing occasionally.
3. Preheat the oven to 450 degrees F.
4. Heat an oven proof skillet in oven for about 15 minutes.
5. Place pork with marinade in heated skillet and bake for about 10 minutes.
6. Remove from oven and toss well.
7. Bake for about 10-15 minutes.
8. Remove from oven and keep aside to cool for about 10 minutes.
9. With a sharp knife slice the pork tenderloin in desired pieces.
10. In a skillet, heat oil on medium heat.
11. Add onion and sauté for about 4-5 minutes.
12. Add garlic and Serrano pepper and sauté for about 1 minute.
13. Add turnip, salt and black pepper and cook for about 3-4 minutes.
14. Divide the turnip noodles in serving plates and top with pork pieces.
15. Garnish with scallion and serve.

Butter Lobster With Sweet Potato

Time: 35 minutes

Servings: 2

Ingredients:

For Lobster:

2 tablespoons olive oil

2 tablespoons butter, melted

2 cloves garlic, minced

1 tablespoon fresh ginger, minced

¼ cup fresh chives, chopped

2 tablespoons Sriracha

Salt, to taste

8-ounce lobster tails

For Sweet Potato:

1 tablespoon olive oil

2 garlic cloves, minced

2 medium sweet potatoes, peeled and spiralized with Blade C

¼ cup chicken broth

Salt and freshly ground black pepper, to taste

2 tablespoons fresh cilantro

2 fresh lemon wedges

Directions:

1. In a large bowl, add olive oil, butter, garlic, ginger, chives, Sriracha, salt and lobster and mix till well combined.

2. Refrigerate, covered for about 3-4 hours.

3. Preheat the grill on high heat.

4. Grease the grill grate.

5. Place the lobster tails on the hot grill, flesh side down.

6. Grill for about 4-5 minutes.

7. Top with fresh cilantro and serve with lemon wedges.

8. Meanwhile in a skillet, heat oil on medium heat.

9. Add garlic and sauté for about 30 seconds.

10. Add sweet potato noodles and cook for about 3-4 minutes.

11. Add broth, salt and black pepper and cook for about 3-4 minutes.

12. Stir in cilantro and remove from the heat.

13. Divide sweet potato noodles in serving plates and top with lobster tails.

14. Serve with lemon wedges.

Zucchini Onion Mussels

Time: 35 minutes

Servings: 4

Ingredients:

1 tablespoon coconut oil

1 cup yellow onion, chopped

2 celery stalks, chopped

2 garlic cloves, minced

2 cups grape tomatoes, halved

¼ teaspoon cayenne pepper

Salt and freshly ground black pepper, to taste

20-24 mussels, scrubbed and debearded

2 tablespoons fresh parsley, chopped

4 zucchinis, spiralized with Blade C

Directions:

1. In a skillet, melt coconut oil on medium heat.
2. Add onion and celery and sauté for about 3-4 minutes.
3. Add garlic and sauté for about 1 minute.
4. Stir in tomatoes and seasoning and cook, covered for about 4-5 minutes.
5. Reduce the heat to low and stir in mussels and parsley.
6. Cook, covered for about 2 minutes.
7. Meanwhile in a pan of boiling water, cook the zucchini noodles for about 2-3 minutes. Drain well.
9. In a large serving bowl, place zucchini noodles.
10. Add mussel mixture and gently stir to combne.

Garlic Crab With Butternut Squash

Time: 25 minutes

Servings: 2

Ingredients:

1 butternut squash, peeled and spiralized with Blade C

3 tablespoons olive oil, divided

Salt and freshly ground black pepper, to taste

1 garlic clove, minced

¾ cup fresh crab meat

¼ teaspoon red pepper flakes, crushed

1 tablespoon fresh cilantro leaves, chopped

Directions:

1. Preheat the oven to 400 degrees F.

2. Lightly, grease a baking sheet.

3. In a large bowl, add butternut squash, 1 tablespoon of oil, salt and black pepper and toss to coat well.

4. Transfer the squash mixture in prepared baking sheet.

5. Bake for about 10 minutes, tossing once after 5 minutes.

6. Transfer the baked butternut squash in serving bowl

7. Meanwhile in a large skillet, heat remaining oil on medium heat.

8. Add garlic and sauté for about 1 minute.

9. Add crab meat and red pepper flakes and cook for about 3 minutes.

10. Place crabmeat mixture over butternut squash.

11. Garnish with cilantro and serve.

Tamari Ginger Cabbage with Ground Pork

Time: 35 minutes

Servings: 4

Ingredients:

1 tablespoon fresh ginger, minced

1 teaspoon garlic, minced

3 tablespoons tamari

1 tablespoon dried oregano, crushed

1½ tablespoons extra virgin olive oil, divided

1 onion, chopped

1 medium head cabbage, spiralized with Blade C

1 pound lean ground pork

4 scallions, chopped

½ cup fresh parsley leaves, chopped

Salt and freshly ground black pepper, to taste

1 tablespoon fresh lemon juice

Directions:

1. In a bowl, mix together, ginger, garlic, tamari and oregano and keep aside.
2. In a large skillet, heat 1 tablespoon of oil on medium heat.
3. Add onion and sauté for about 4-5 minutes.
4. Add cabbage and half of ginger mixture and cook for about 2-3 minutes.
5. Transfer the cabbage mixture into a large serving bowl.
6. In the same skillet, heat remaining oil on medium heat.
7. Add pork and remaining ginger mixture and cook for about 8-10 minutes.
8. Stir in scallions, parsley and seasoning and cook for about 2 minutes.
9. Transfer the pork mixture into bowl with cabbage and gently too to mix.
10. Drizzle with lemon juice and serve.

Conclusion

Thank you again for downloading this book!

I hope you've found this book creative, Healthy and delicious, and hopefully after this, you will master your spiralizer technique

If you enjoyed this book, then I'd like to ask you for a favor, would you be kind enough to leave a review for this book on Amazon? It'd be greatly appreciated!

Thank you and good luck!

Made in the USA
Lexington, KY
13 August 2017